Praise for *Cholesterol Protection For Life*

Dr. Fuhrman's *Cholesterol Protection For Life* is a no-nonsense, how-to, right-to-the-point book for cholesterol lowering and eliminating heart disease. Dr. Fuhrman's extraordinary depth of hands-on experience enables him to speak with authority about strategies for achieving a healthful life and avoiding chronic disease. Its simplicity will guide an inquiring public, and its clarity of message will assist health practitioners.

Caldwell B. Esselstyn, Jr., M.D.
Preventive Cardiology Consultant
Department of General Surgery, Cleveland Clinic

In this fascinating book, Dr. Fuhrman tells you the most effective way to lower cholesterol without drugs and how to virtually disease-proof your body. It will show you how to kick your heart disease-promoting diet and lifestyle habits and adopt an exquisitely enjoyable anti-aging way of life. Follow Dr. Fuhrman's easy-to-understand formula in this book and start having the best and healthiest time of your life.

Gerald Deutsch, President
National Health Association

Cholesterol Protection For Life does an outstanding job of presenting a very complex topic in a clear and orderly fashion. This book is a timely piece of work and one that can be a very useful tool for the reduction of not only cardiovascular disease, but most other forms of chronic illnesses in our society. A must read for anyone with an interest in their personal health or the health of a loved one.

Baxter Montgomery, M.D., FACC
Clinical Assistant Professor of Medicine
The University of Texas Health Science Center, Houston
President of Houston Cardiac Association and HCA Wellness

My cholesterol used to be over 200! I was "a heart attack waiting to happen." Thanks to Dr Fuhrman's *Cholesterol Protection For Life,* my total cholesterol is now 142. I'm thrilled. I feel healthier just knowing I'm safe, and I look so much better!

Denise Viscanza

My cholesterol dropped dramatically, my angina resolved, and my heart condition vanished. I take no medications anymore. Dr. Fuhrman saved my life.

wlikowski

D1153886

CHOLESTEROL
PROTECTION
For
LIFE

Other books by
Joel Fuhrman, M.D.

EAT TO LIVE–
The Revolutionary Formula for
Fast and Sustained Weight Loss

DISEASE-PROOF YOUR CHILD–
Feeding Kids Right

FASTING AND EATING FOR HEALTH–
A Medical Doctor's Program for Conquering Disease

CHOLESTEROL PROTECTION

For LIFE

JOEL FUHRMAN, M.D.

ᵍᵍᵉ

Gift of Health Press

Contact:
Joel Fuhrman, M.D., P.C.
4 Walter E. Foran Boulevard, Suite 409
Flemington, N J 08822
(908) 237-0200
www.DrFuhrman.com.

Printed in the United States of America

ISBN: 0-974463-32-9
ISBN-13: 978-0974463-32-2

Library of Congress Control Number: 2006924420

Publisher's Note
Keep in mind that results vary from person to person. Some people have a medical history and/or condition that may warrant individualized recommendation and, in some cases, drugs and even surgery. Do not start, stop, or change medication without professional medical advice, and do not change your diet if you are ill or on medication, except under the supervision of a competent physician. Neither this, nor any other book, is intended to take the place of personalized medical care or treatment.

For reasons of privacy, the names of patients have been changed.

Book design by Jim Lennon, Lennon Media, Inc.

10 09 08 07 06 • 9 8 7 6 5 4 3 2 1

Dedicated to my family–
Lisa, Talia, Jenna, Cara, and Sean

Acknowledgements

I want to acknowledge the people who helped me prepare this new edition, especially my wife, Lisa. Not only did she edit, revise, and offer terrific suggestions, she also created many of the delicious menus and recipes you'll find in this book.

Robin Jeep, an incomparable celebrity chef, also contributed a batch of incredible new recipes. Robin has traveled the world over preparing gourmet meals for the rich and famous. Now that she is specializing in the cuisine of nutritional excellence, food lovers are learning that healthful eating does not have to take a backseat to taste and pleasure. After you've eaten a few of Robin's superb recipes, you'll wonder why you ever thought that self-discipline or denial had anything to do with achieving vibrant health and long life.

My good friend Jim Lennon edited and designed this new edition, and I am grateful to have access to his thoughtful suggestions.

I want to acknowledge the comments and suggestions from my doctor friends and also to thank all the physicians who refer their heart patients to me for nutritional intervention, and to the many others who use this book in their medical practices.

Special thanks goes to all the people who have allowed me to tell their case histories in this book. I have changed their names to accommodate their privacy.

Contents

Foreword xiii

Introduction 1

1. Lowering Cholesterol Saves Lives 11
2. Medical Approaches to Cholesterol and Heart Health. . . 19
3. Heart Attack Prevention that Actually Works 31
4. Dietary Mistakes to Avoid 43
5. A Heart-Protective Diet 59
6. Dietary Guidelines for Lowering Cholesterol 73
7. Menus and Recipes 85
8. Dietary Supplements that Lower Cholesterol. 115
9. Frequently Asked Questions 127
10. A Strategy for Success. 141

References 149

Index. 157

About the Author 160

Foreword

The United States Surgeon General, Vice Admiral Richard H. Carmona, M.D., M.P.H., F.A.C.S., eloquently expressed the dire position of health in the United States:

"As a society, we can no longer afford to make poor health choices such as being physically inactive and eating an unhealthy diet; these choices have led to a tremendous obesity epidemic. As policy makers and health professionals, we must embrace small steps toward coordinated policy and environmental changes that will help Americans live longer, better, healthier lives."

Despite the obvious warning signs, we continue to ignore the reality of our skyrocketing health problems. Our health system (focusing as it does on treatment rather than prevention) relies on an ever-expanding armamentarium of medications, tests, and procedures that fail to address the primary cause of our escalating ill health—the way we choose to eat and live. There has been a staggering increase in nutritionally-caused diseases, which are now the largest cause of death throughout the world. In 2002, ischemic heart disease and stroke accounted for 17 million deaths worldwide, followed by cancer (7 million), chronic lung diseases (4 million), and diabetes mellitus (1 million). Careful analysis shows that the common denominators among the leading causes of death are tobacco and alcohol use, lack of physical activity, and unhealthful diets. In other words, the major causes of death are controlled by our individual lifestyle choices, with diet playing a preeminent role.

It is sad that in our modern age of science, dietary ignorance still is such a major contributor to the development of disease. Despite the initial efforts by the FDA, the American Heart Association, and other national panels' and organizations' guidelines to recommend healthful diets, there has been a dramatic increase in obesity since 1999. In fact, over 30% of adults are obese. Shockingly, of children and adolescents between ages six and nineteen, 16% are considered overweight. Knowing the role that obesity plays in the development of heart disease, cancer, and diabetes, it is not shocking that the annual cost of obesity in the United States alone in the year 2000 was $117 billion. We are facing an epidemic.

As a cardiologist and director of a secondary prevention program for patients who already have suffered some form of heart disease, I deal with the psychosocial aspects of changing behavior daily. To make permanent, positive change, patients must overcome the hurdle of denial and reach a level of frustration that motivates them to want to take control over their health. Unfortunately, today's system of conventional care simply does not effectively support patients' efforts—very little accurate information is available about nutrition.

The fact that you have picked up a copy of Dr. Fuhrman's book tells me that you are ready to go beyond conventional care and take *all the steps necessary* to get your health back. I have good news for you. Multiple studies have demonstrated that the plant-based diet program Dr. Fuhrman recommends produces dramatic results. What's more, *Cholesterol Protection for Life* makes eating and preparing that diet attainable and accessible, easy and understandable. I applaud your commitment to take responsibility for your diet and health.

If recent experience is any indication, we cannot rely on government institutions and policy makers to take the lead in raising awareness of the importance of diet in the development of disease. Unless we want to join millions of Americans who are getting fatter, more unfit, and more unhealthy, we need to seek out high-quality diet and health information like that which Dr. Fuhrman provides.

The American Heart Association revised its dietary guidelines in 2000 to include more plant-based food and to further reduce the intake of saturated fat and cholesterol. Multiple studies have demonstrated the role of high-saturated fat diets in the development of heart disease and other diseases, and it has been demonstrated that plant-based diets can bring remarkable benefits. In fact, medical studies have demonstrated that there is a significantly greater reduction in LDL cholesterol on a plant-based diet compared with the standard low-fat diet recommended by traditional health authorities.

Dr. Fuhrman is way ahead of his time. His years of painstaking research have enabled him to develop an insightful and effective dietary approach to treating his patients. He began using nutritional excellence as a successful therapeutic modality long before there was even a cursory understanding of its importance in the fields of medicine or governmental policy.

The economic cost of heart disease and other chronic disease is staggering. Health care costs increased over 50% between 2000 and 2005, and the nation's economy is being weighted down by out-of-control costs that are bankrupting businesses and sending jobs overseas. The average cost to a traditional health insurer for the first ninety days after a heart attack is $38,500.

While economic woes are an obvious concern, the personal tragedy that accompanies illness is incalculable. The suffering from illnesses and from witnessing the suffering of loved ones extracts a steep personal cost. What makes this collective family pain so difficult to deal with as a cardiologist and a healer is the knowledge that most diseases are the result of factors that could have been addressed through simple diet and lifestyle changes. Dr. Fuhrman firmly but gently tells us how to make these lifesaving changes, enabling us to learn how to protect our lives and the lives of ones we love.

Suzanne R. Steinbaum, D.O.
Medical Director, Center for Cardiac Health
Beth Israel Medical Center, New York City

Introduction

This year, more than 1.5 million people will have a heart attack, and about 1 million will die from heart disease (one every 30 seconds). Heart disease and strokes kill more people than all other causes of death combined.

The direct medical costs of heart disease have been measured at roughly $60 billion per year, which is more than any other medical condition. But that is only the beginning. How do we measure the pain, suffering, and emotional distress thrust upon individuals and families as a result of this staggering epidemic of broken hearts?

The purpose of this book is to teach you why heart disease is raging out of control, and what you must do to ensure that it will not ensnare you or your loved ones. Heart disease is almost entirely preventable, and you can make yourself virtually heart attack-proof. Even if you already have heart disease, you most likely can recover and lead a rich and rewarding life.

How can I be so confident that you can beat heart disease?

The three main reasons are these:

1. During my 15 years of experience working with high-risk heart patients, I have counseled hundreds of patients with advanced heart disease, many of whom had angina and were told they needed urgent bypass surgery or angioplasty.

All of them improved their heart conditions—and *none* of them ever had a heart attack.

2. During Dr. Caldwell Esselstyn's 17-year research with a group of advanced heart disease patients, *no one who followed his advice had a heart attack.*[1]

3. Cultures around the world that eat diets rich in vegetables have no recorded heart disease.[2] In fact, there are areas in rural China where there has *never been a single documented case of heart attack.*[3]

You might wonder if it is possible for a person to faithfully follow my advice—to the letter—and still experience a heart attack. I suppose it is possible, but it hasn't happened yet. Based on my experience and the overwhelming weight of scientific evidence, I am convinced that if you follow my advice, it simply won't happen. Obviously, risk goes down gradually over time. I am not claiming that following the program described in this book for a week or even a month will offer total heart attack protection. But as months pass and you adhere to my heart-protective program, I am reasonably certain that the chances of experiencing a heart attack will become incredibly slim.

Cholesterol and heart disease

The risk of cardiovascular disease, resulting in a heart attack or embolic stroke, is directly related to your cholesterol level. High LDL cholesterol (the so-called "bad" cholesterol) is a significant indication that you are at high risk of a heart attack. That is why today's cardiac-protective recommendations are:

- *Keep LDL cholesterol below 100 mg/dL.*
- *Keep total cholesterol below 150 mg/dL.*

Unfortunately, fewer than 10% of all adult Americans meet this requirement, and some high-risk individuals need to keep their cholesterol at even lower levels.

It is important to keep in mind that while high cholesterol is a key risk factor for heart disease, it is not the only one. Even if new drugs were developed that could lower your cholesterol level *safely* into the recommended range, you still could be vulnerable to heart attack if you didn't address other critical risk factors simultaneously. These additional risk factors are primarily related to poor diet and lack of physical activity. This book will teach you how to address those factors, as well.

The best news is that you are not going to be dependent on any magical medication or surgical procedure for your health and recovery. You will be *earning* your heart health by following my easy-to-understand program of nutritional excellence. The chapters that follow will tell you exactly what you need to do and how to do it. (And the recipe chapter will show you that you don't have to sacrifice great taste to achieve great health.)

Drugs not the answer

In the United States, the standard approach to treating and preventing (if you can call it that) heart disease is to prescribe pills, medical procedures, and/or surgery, depending upon the condition of the patient. For decades, the medical/pharmaceutical industry has kept profits high by claiming to be "searching for a cure" and "providing the best care money can buy." But little has been accomplished besides creating a growing demand for high-tech, expensive, and largely ineffective treatments. Medical costs and insurance rates have skyrocketed—and so has heart disease. The entire scheme has been a colossal failure.

The main problem with using drugs to lower cholesterol (aside from the risky side effects) is that drugs give patients a false sense of security. As their cholesterol levels go down, patients mistakenly think they are protected against heart disease. As a result, they continue to eat the same disease-causing diet that caused the heart disease—and the risk of heart attack—in the first place. Little do they know that they still are at risk of suffering a heart attack or a stroke.

Cholesterol-lowering drugs only reduce your risk of heart attack by about 30%. On a population-based level, that may be significant; reducing the number of Americans who experience heart attacks by 30% is fantastic. But on an individual level, it simply is not good enough. I don't know about you, but I don't want to reduce my risk of heart attack by a mere 30%. I want to reduce it by 100%. I don't want to have to worry about it at all. But the only way to accomplish that feat is by permanently and conscientiously putting into practice the recommendations in this book.

Fortunately for you and your loved ones, an overwhelming number of peer-reviewed scientific papers have shown that there is an inexpensive, safe, and effective way to prevent and reverse heart disease. This research—along with my many years of experience with patients—forms the foundation of the program I describe in this book. Finally, there is an alternative to the financially devastating and futile medical/pharmaceutical approach. Once people learn about it—and incorporate it into their eating and living patterns—we will begin to see heart disease disappear entirely.

Reducing other risk factors

What makes the approach I spell out in this book so superior to even the most elaborate medical care (i.e., extraordinarily risky and expensive care) is that by adopting a program of nutritional excellence, you not only lower your LDL cholesterol, you eliminate other risk factors at the same time.

Following my approach, you will:

- *dramatically lower concentration of CRP (C-Reactive Protein);*
- *assure that your homocysteine level is favorable;*
- *lower your weight and waist measurements;*
- *lower your blood pressure;*
- *lower your fasting glucose;*
- *improve your antioxidant and nutrient levels.*

Tragically, most patients are not given the facts they need to truly protect themselves against heart attacks. Instead, they are told that it is okay to eat the heart disease-causing American diet as long as they sprinkle a few drugs on top to try to lessen the risk a bit. I consider this to be bad medicine and predict that in the future, failure to give patients the up-to-date scientific information they need will be considered malpractice.

If every physician in America gave patients the powerful information contained in this book, we would have a wonderful new problem—patients would get well, most doctors and hospitals could close their doors, and the lucrative pharmaceutical industry would collapse. Doctors would need to retrain themselves for new careers in other fields.

Five success stories
In my medical practice, I have helped thousands of patients successfully lower their cholesterol levels without drugs. Almost all of my patients prefer this conservative approach, and it is very rare that they are not able to achieve these protective levels naturally. In cases

where patients reject my recommended approach, I encourage them to lower their cholesterol as much as possible through natural methods and to use prescription drugs only when absolutely necessary (in order to minimize the potentially serious side effects of the drugs).

To give you an example of a typical day in my medical practice, I recently had follow-up appointments with five patients who have successfully dropped their LDL cholesterol below or near 100 mg/dL.

At the time these patients began following my recommendations, not only did each have dangerously high cholesterol levels, they had numerous other health problems as well. Peggy suffered from chronic anemia. Eugene was tired all of the time. Keith had chronic heartburn and allergies. Maria had become severely ill from a statin drug prescribed to her by her prior physician. Peter had angina and could not walk half a block without chest pain.

Fortunately, each of them was eager to do whatever it took to get well, and they all knew from personal experience that prescription drugs were risky and not an effective answer. They had been on my nutritional excellence program for six to eight weeks when they returned to my office for checkups. This is what we found.

Peggy:	Before	After
Total Cholesterol	249	150
Triglycerides	169	105
LDL	157	80
HDL	58	49
Eugene:		
Total Cholesterol	247	156
Triglycerides	72	42
LDL	191	104
HDL	51	44

	Before	*After*
Keith:		
Total Cholesterol	237	158
Triglycerides	165	79
LDL	152	99
HDL	52	43.5
Maria:		
Total Cholesterol	283	168
Triglycerides	90	79
LDL	183	98
HDL	91	52
Peter:	(on Zocor)	(off Zocor)
Total Cholesterol	164	126
Tryglycerides	210	179
LDL	119	54
HDL	32	36

The results clearly showed that all five eliminated their cardio-vascular high-risk status. Many of their other problems cleared up as well. Peggy's anemia went away. Eugene was no longer fatigued. Keith's heartburn went away, he stopped his antacids and acid-blocking medication, and his allergies started to improve. Peter's angina was gone, and he was walking over 2.5 miles per day without any pain. They all were thrilled that their symptoms melted away so quickly after only a few weeks of following my nutritional advice. Perhaps most importantly, in addition to the specific health benefits each patient experienced, they all developed a renewed enthusiasm about life.

Total health improvement

When you adopt a program of nutritional excellence to reverse or prevent heart disease, you get the added benefit of preventing and reversing almost all other diseases simultaneously. For example, your digestion will improve. You'll get rid of your heartburn, hemorrhoids, and constipation. Your headaches will disappear. You'll have more energy, age more slowly, and lower your risk of other serious diseases—especially dementia, strokes, diabetes, and cancer.

Admittedly, some patients initially find it difficult to switch from a low-nutrient, dairy-meat-refined-carbohydrate-based diet to a high-nutrient, vegetable-fruit-based one. But this difficulty is temporary. In time, patients report that they enjoy eating the new way, discovering new tastes and aromas, and treasuring their newfound energy.

Please don't think that you have to be a patient of mine to get great results. Thousands of people read my books (and learn from the member center on my website: www.DrFuhrman.com), and I regularly receive e-mails and letters from people who want to tell me their success stories. The letter on page 9 is a typical one.

Cholesterol protection and more

My goal with this book is to enable you to achieve the recommended cardiac-protective cholesterol levels, while eating delicious food and enjoying life without a dependence on medications. The approach is twofold: Combine the most powerful dietary program with the strongest natural cholesterol-reducing supplements.

First, I describe an eating plan that will dramatically lower your cholesterol. This nutritional information gives you the tools you need to take control of your health. My dietary program (the scientific basis of which is explained in greater depth in my book *Eat to Live*) provides a formula that has helped thousands of people:

- *lower cholesterol;*
- *lose weight;*

Dear Dr. Fuhrman,

I am one happy 68-year-old. I enjoyed relatively good health for much of my life. However, in recent years, I've struggled with high blood pressure (160/105) and high cholesterol (275). My cardiologist visit last October resulted in his wanting to increase my Lipitor from 10mg/day to 20mg/day. Also, he wanted to place me on Accupril. I told him that I had recently bought your book *Eat to Live,* and that I was going to make a major diet change and follow your recommendations instead. I have been following your program with spectacular results, and I have been able to stop all medications. I saw my cardiologist yesterday with the following blood work results:

Total Cholesterol	148
HDL	62
Ratio	2.4
Triglycerides	85
LDL	69

While my weight had been constant since high school at 235 pounds (I am 6'6" tall), I currently weigh 211 pounds and feel the best I have in a long time. My wife and I cook most days in a Crock-Pot. Yes, we make a lot of soups with collard greens, mustard greens, spinach, beans, etc. I tell everyone who will listen that there is no "free lunch" and that you have to stay focused and committed.

I took a copy of your book with me to my cardiologist. He said that he had heard of your program. He also said that I had made a remarkable turnaround and should be proud of myself, which I am.

I want to thank you for my greatly improved health.

Sincerely yours,

Joseph Lavaler

- *boost immune function;*
- *lower high blood pressure;*
- *reverse adult-onset (Type II) diabetes;*
- *achieve normal bowel function;*
- *reverse and prevent autoimmune diseases;*
- *maintain youthful vigor;*
- *slow the aging process.*

The second part of the *Cholesterol Protection for Life* plan describes nutritional supplements that can add to the cholesterol-lowering effect of my high-nutrient diet. I usually recommend a few natural cholesterol-lowering substances for the patients who do not find that dietary excellence alone is sufficient to bring their cholesterol levels down to the most protective range.

If you follow my dietary recommendations and also take the recommended natural cholesterol-lowering agents, you will see a huge difference in your cholesterol levels after just one month. As time progresses, you will see even further improvement. Regular exercise can provide additional benefits.

For the greatest benefits, I urge you to start implementing both parts of the *Cholesterol Protection for Life* program today.

Lowering Cholesterol Saves Lives

It has been well established that high cholesterol levels are associated with increased risk of coronary heart disease and that lowering your LDL cholesterol sufficiently offers powerful protection against heart disease. Research has shown that heart attacks are entirely preventable, and that heart disease is both preventable and reversible through aggressive, cholesterol-lowering nutritional intervention.

There is a direct correlation between cholesterol levels and heart attack risk at total cholesterol levels above 150 mg/dL. As your total cholesterol level rises over this baseline, the risk of death from heart attack increases proportionally. Shockingly, over 95% of all Americans, Canadians, and Europeans have cholesterol levels above 150 mg/dL. The average cholesterol level in America is a whopping 208 mg/dL, which means that the average American has an unacceptably high risk of sudden death.

Most heart attacks occur in the 175-225 mg/dL range, but don't think that getting your total cholesterol below 175 mg/dL is the solution. In the famous Framingham study, 35% of heart disease occurred in those with total cholesterol levels in the range of 150-200 mg/dL, and the only levels where no heart disease deaths occurred were below 150 mg/dL.[4]

What are the optimal cholesterol levels?

According to the National Cholesterol Education Program Adult Treatment Panel III, the target LDL cholesterol for patients with heart disease is below 100 mg/dL. The European guidelines set the LDL cholesterol level below 115 mg/dL. But, as you will see, even these levels may be too high for a great many people.

Describing optimal cholesterol levels is a complex task. However, one general concept is important to grasp—in otherwise healthy individuals, lower is better. Another thing to keep in mind is that your cholesterol level is not the only factor associated with the development of atherosclerosis. Atherosclerosis is a complex process involving a myriad of risk factors, including low antioxidant intake, excess caloric consumption, and lack of adequate exercise.

The heart disease epidemic is a modern phenomenon that is intricately entwined with the plentiful availability of low-cost, low-nutrient food everywhere in the developed world. There is no evidence that early humans developed heart disease or atherosclerosis, even those who reached seventy and eighty years of age.[5] Early humans had a total cholesterol range of 90-150 mg/dL and an LDL cholesterol range of 50-75 mg/dL.

The chart at right shows the total cholesterol levels of various humans living today, as well as those of two near-relative primates living in the wild. As you can see, cholesterol levels of modern Westernized humans are about

Average total cholesterol in animals and humans[6]

Baboon	*110 mg/dL*
Howler monkey	*100 mg/dL*
Pygmy tribes (humans)	*100 mg/dL*
Hazda tribes (humans)	*110 mg/dL*
Rural Chinese	*125 mg/dL*
Adult Americans	*208 mg/dL*

twice as high as the normal physiologic levels observed in infants, wild animals, and primitive populations eating uncultivated, natural foods. Healthy human infants typically have LDL cholesterol in the 30-70 mg/dL range.

The lower, the better

Recent interventional trials on cholesterol lowering in modern humans found the further you push the LDL cholesterol down, the larger the degree of regression of coronary artery disease observed.[7] In other words, lowering the LDL cholesterol to 80 mg/dL showed a reversal of disease in most participants, whereas lowering the LDL cholesterol to 110 mg/dL did not. In fact, the scientists observed a *worsening* in the overall atheroma volume in the participants who only lowered their LDL cholesterol to 110 mg/dL.[8]

Most of these trials demonstrated the inadequacy of LDL cholesterol reduction to current goals of 100 mg/dL. If you combine the data from all of these studies, you find that to get to the level where the cardiac event rate approaches zero, LDL cholesterol must be down in the 50-70 mg/dL range.

Two studies showed that even an LDL cholesterol level slightly below 100 mg/dL is not ideal, and that lower levels bring added benefits. Researchers took patients who had already achieved an average LDL cholesterol of about 95-100 mg/dL and added additional medication, driving patients' LDL cholesterol levels down to the 60-65 mg/dL range. The results showed a 25% further reduction in heart disease incidence.[9]

Since the total effect of dramatic LDL cholesterol reduction is so profound (for example, blood vessel inflammation and vessel function have been shown to improve as LDL cholesterol is lowered to below 70 mg/dL), it is reasonable to theorize that a) the atherosclerosis process is dependent upon LDL cholesterol rising above a certain threshold, and that b) extremely low LDL cholesterol may prevent coronary heart events regardless of other risk factors.

Researchers in the field gradually are adopting the position that the truly optimal LDL cholesterols are below 80 mg/dL. The current target of 100 mg/dL is a great first step, considering how far most Americans are above that. But for those who have heart disease and who want to maximally reverse it, a better goal would be to get LDL cholesterol below 70 mg/dL. It could mean the difference between life and death.

Keep in mind that it is impossible to drive LDL cholesterol this low with conventional eating or dieting (i.e., the SAD, standard American diet), and the studies referenced above relied on cholesterol-lowering drugs. The only way to achieve cholesterol levels in the 50-70 mg/dL without taking drugs is to use the vegetable-based dietary approach described in this book and to take supplements that contain the natural cholesterol-lowering substances I describe in Chapter 8.

It is crucial to understand the limitations of drug therapy. Most studies documenting the benefits of cholesterol-lowering drugs only show benefits for patients who already have heart disease. In these studies, investigators found significant improvement in overall mortality for people who already had significant heart disease. However, when utilizing drugs to lower the cholesterol of people at lower risk of heart disease, statistically significant life-span benefits were not observed. The potential long-term dangers of the drugs may offset the cholesterol-lowering (cardiac) benefits. For example, in one study, 22 fewer deaths from vascular disease were offset by an increase of 24 deaths from cancer.[10] Utilizing high doses and combinations of drugs to achieve the maximum protection and reversal of heart disease is not without risk.

For healthy individuals who practice nutritional excellence, exercise regularly, and do not have heart problems, an LDL cholesterol goal of 100 mg/dL is sufficient. Utilizing drugs to drive LDL cholesterol down to a level below 70 mg/dL in such individuals would be unwise and unnecessary. The program of nutritional excellence described in this book brings with it substantial cardiovascular benefits independent of the cholesterol-lowering effects. These include optimizing intracellular biochemistry; reducing intravascular inflammation; lowering blood sugar, blood pressure, and cholesterol; and supplying disease-protective nutrients that enable cellular repair mechanisms. Heart disease would be incredibly unusual in a population following this program. Adopting nutritional excellence—and becoming slim and physically fit—offer powerful protection against heart disease at every cholesterol level.

New guidelines for physicians

As a result of the recent clinical trials, new clinical guidelines on cholesterol lowering have been released that advise physicians to treat high-risk heart patients more aggressively. These new cholesterol guidelines have been endorsed by the American Heart Association, the American College of Cardiology, and the National Heart, Lung, and Blood Institute.[11] The guidelines categorize people based on their perceived risk of having a heart attack in the next ten years and recommend cholesterol goals for each risk category. Physicians are advised to use an LDL cholesterol goal below 70 mg/dL when treating patients with a very high risk of heart disease. The complete list of all categories appears in the chart below.

As an example of how categories were defined, a very-high-risk patient would be one with known coronary artery disease plus multiple risk factors, such as diabetes, high blood pressure, and/or cigarette smoking.

Target cholesterol goals for all risk categories

Risk category	LDL goal
Very high	<70 mg/dL
High	<100 mg/dL
Moderately high	<130 mg/dL
Moderate	<130 mg/dL
Low	<160 mg/dL

These new guidelines, though a step in the right direction, still do not take cholesterol lowering to the level that clinical trial data supports for our general population. The new guidelines only lower the LDL cholesterol goals for high- and very-high-risk heart patients, not everyone else. The reason for this is that the benefits of cholesterol-lowering medication in lower-risk populations have to be weighed against the cost and potential dose-related side effects of medications that would be needed to reach those goals. As a result, most of the population will be kept at risk simply because the conventional medical/pharmaceutical industry does not have the means to safely lower cholesterol in this group.

More protective guidelines

While I agree with the decision to lower the LDL cholesterol goal to 70 mg/dL for persons at considerable risk of a heart attack, I strongly disagree with the decision to allow other people to walk around with LDL cholesterol levels in the range of 100-160 mg/dL. Based on the research, many of these people are heart attacks waiting to happen, and their first coronary event might very well be their last.

My guidelines are much more protective than those of the American Heart Association and the other groups because the methods I use to achieve heart-healthy goals are different. Since I use a healthful, natural approach to reach the most protective levels (rather than relying on drugs), I can extend the protection to the entire population, not just those at high risk of dying of a heart attack. When you drive the LDL cholesterol below 100 mg/dL with drugs, you *reduce* risk; but when you drive it down with nutritional excellence, you *eliminate* risk.

In addition, by maximizing results with ample consumption of green vegetables and other nutrient-rich foods, you enhance your overall health. So, not only do you reduce (or eliminate) your likelihood of heart attack and stroke, you also dramatically reduce your chances of developing cancer, dementia, macular degeneration, arthritis, diabetes, osteoporosis, and other typical degenerative diseases. That is why cholesterol lowering through nutritional excellence is the only choice for well-informed individuals.

Medical Approaches to Cholesterol and Heart Health

To achieve the peace of mind that comes with knowing that you are virtually heart disease-proof, you must lower your cholesterol levels far below what most people (and even many doctors) consider healthful. Just a few years ago, physicians were telling patients that levels below 200 mg/dL were satisfactory. Today, we know that a much lower cholesterol level is needed to be truly safe.

The latest recommendation from most medical authorities and medical organizations is to get your LDL cholesterol level below 100 mg/dL, and even lower if you are at high risk. This new recommendation came about based on the results of numerous epidemiological studies. It is now clear that people in countries where a simple, plant-based diet is the norm do not suffer heart attacks, and those populations have much lower cholesterol levels than would have been considered acceptable in the past. For example, the average total cholesterol in rural China is 127 mg/dL, and the average LDL cholesterol is below 80 mg/dL. Heart attacks in rural China are exceedingly rare. Similar findings have been observed in multiple interventional and population studies, such as the Harvard Health Study; individuals whose LDL cholesterol levels were below 100 mg/dL did not suffer heart attacks.

With near unanimous recognition of the importance of maintaining LDL cholesterol levels below 100 mg/dL, medical authorities have started to recommend cholesterol-lowering drugs for the vast majority of Americans. Not only are drugs not a panacea, they also can produce troublesome and even dangerous side effects. Why expose yourself to those risks?

Drugs seem to work

Based on the results of studies like the three described below, it is easy to see why so many doctors are enthusiastic about cholesterol-lowering medication.

A 1994 study called the Scandinavian Simvastatin Survival Study found that lowering cholesterol can prevent heart attacks and significantly reduce death in men and women who already have heart disease and high cholesterol. For over five years, more than 4,400 patients with heart disease and total cholesterol levels of 213-310 mg/dL were given either a cholesterol-lowering drug or a placebo. The drug they were given is known as a statin, and it reduced total cholesterol levels by 25% and LDL cholesterol levels by 35%. The study found that in those receiving statin drugs, deaths from heart disease were reduced by 42%, the chance of having a nonfatal heart attack was reduced by 37%, and the need for bypass surgery or angioplasty was reduced by 37%.

In 1996, the results of the Cholesterol and Recurrent Events (CARE) Study showed the benefits of cholesterol lowering in patients with heart disease. This study reported that even in patients with seemingly normal cholesterol levels (average of 209 mg/dL), cholesterol lowering with a statin drug lowered the risk of having another heart attack or dying by 24%. These patients also were less likely to need bypass surgery (26% reduction) or angioplasty (22% reduction) during the study. Women benefited even more than men, reducing their risk of having another heart attack by 45%.

A study published in 1998, the Long-Term Intervention with Pravastatin in Ischaemic Disease (LIPID) study, examined the effects of cholesterol lowering in people with heart disease (those who already had experienced a heart attack or had been hospitalized for angina) who had relatively average cholesterol levels. The LIPID study used a statin drug to lower cholesterol levels in the treatment group. All study participants were counseled about following a cholesterol-lowering diet. The LIPID results showed that a drop of 18% in total cholesterol and 25% in LDL cholesterol produced a 24% decrease in deaths from heart attacks among the treatment group compared with the control group. Similarly, cholesterol lowering in the treatment group reduced the overall death rate by 22%, heart attacks by 29%, the need for bypass surgery or angioplasty by 20%, and stroke by 19%.

Since less than 10% of the adult population in America has cholesterol levels that meet the newest recommendations,[12] it would be foolish to dismiss any serious attempt to help people maintain LDL cholesterol levels below 100 mg/dL and total cholesterol below 150 mg/dL. But attempting to achieve these results primarily through the use of medication is questionable.

When patients elect drug intervention rather than dietary modifications, problems can arise, which may increase their risk of premature death. These patients also are at risk of serious side effects from the medication. The known side effects for various statins (the most popular and effective medications to lower cholesterol)

include hepatitis, jaundice, and other liver problems; gastrointesti-
nal upsets; muscle problems; and a variety of blood complications,
such as reduced platelet levels and anemia.

As I will describe, a program of dietary excellence that includes
appropriate supplementation offers the same protection against
heart disease as medication—and more. Since medication does
not address the primary dietary causes of heart disease (which also
are the causes of other disease conditions, most notably cancer),
the potential for achieving additional health benefits is lost. If people were advised to adopt dietary excellence rather than resorting
to drugs, we effectively could reduce both heart attacks and other
chronic conditions at the same time.

Invasive procedures not effective

As seemingly miraculous as they are, bypass surgery and angioplasty are not panaceas. They do not restore the patient's heart to a
healthy state. They are merely attempts to treat various small seg-
ments of diseased hearts, and any benefits they provide are usually only temporary.

To understand the very limited usefulness of bypass surgery
and angioplasty, you need to be aware of the complex nature of
heart disease. The most important thing to understand is that atherosclerotic plaque blankets *all* the vessels in the heart, not just
the ones where the plaque is detectable by angiograms. Bypassing
and/or removing only the most diseased ("clogged") vessels does
not address the very serious risks associated with all of the shallow
and non-obstructive lipid deposits in the vessels that aren't "clogged." The vast majority of patients who undergo these interventions do not experience fewer new heart attacks or achieve longer

survival,[13] and the procedures themselves expose the patients to additional risks of new heart attacks, strokes, infection, encephalopathy, and death.

Since bypass and angioplasty only treat the symptoms and do not address the causes of the disease, it is not surprising that patients experience disease progression, graft shutdown, and restenosis, and need additional procedures as their heart disease (unnecessarily) continues to advance. The vast majority of treated patients die prematurely from heart disease because their disease remains essentially untreated.[14] As a result, the use of surgical and other high-tech interventions, rather than aggressive nutritional intervention, has proven a deadly failure.

Atherosclerosis is a dietary-induced disease. Even if surgical and other high-tech intervention could remove the vast accumulation of plaque throughout the heart that currently goes untreated, unless the patient adopted the dietary program I recommend, coronary artery disease would reoccur quickly. At present, these marginally effective medical interventions are combined with the dangerously ineffective and inaccurate dietary advice given by most doctors and dieticians—to reduce fat and cholesterol and eat less red meat and more chicken and fish. Is it any wonder that bypass and angioplasty patients suffer so many (predictable) subsequent cardiac tragedies?

Numerous studies have demonstrated that the typical dietary recommendations offered by the American Heart Association—to hold cholesterol to less than 200 mg per day and to reduce dietary fat to less than 30%—do not prevent or reverse heart disease.[15] The nutritional causes of heart disease go far beyond the simplistic question of how much less fat to eat. The misguided notion that it is prudent to "eat everything in moderation" leads to tens of thousands of sudden, "unexpected" (at least by most people and their doctors) heart attack deaths. Unless Americans and others who eat low-nutrient, animal-based diets make dramatic changes—and quickly, the heart disease crisis is only going to get worse.

Why heart attacks occur

Heart attacks result from a defect in the plaque wall, which leads to a thrombus (blood clot). Even a small coating of vulnerable plaque, invisible to standard cardiac testing, can (and typically does) cause a heart attack. Individuals without major blockages of their great vessels—such as those who have only 30-50% stenosis (narrowing)—are even more likely to develop a fatal cardiac event than those with more significant blockages.[16]

It is important to note that neither stress tests nor angiography would have identified these people as having heart disease. Stress testing (without imaging) only identifies blockages that obstruct greater than 85% of the vessel lumen (open channel). Being told that your stress test is "normal" is essentially meaningless. It certainly does not mean you do not have significant heart disease or that you won't have a heart attack in the near future. Even coronary catheterization (angiography) does not identify the smaller non-occluding atherosclerotic deposits. Consequently, interventional strategies are not used to treat patients with shallower lesions, in spite of the fact that these are the people who suffer the most heart attacks.

It is not the extent of the blockage that determines your risk; it is the vulnerability of the plaque and its propensity to rupture. In fact, 70-80% of all myocardial infarctions (heart attacks) are caused by plaque that is not obstructive or visible on angiography or stress tests.

When athromas (lipid deposits) first develop on the wall of a blood vessel, the walls remodel outward, preserving the lumen. These are the most vulnerable or lethal plaques, and they do not obstruct or encroach on the blood flow. These heart attack-prone lesions have dangerous characteristics that are not revealed by cardiac angiography or catheterization.

Inflammatory cells and a large lipid core of cholesterol in the plaques are characteristic of the most dangerous lesions. The breakage or rupture of these vulnerable lesions causes heart attacks. Cardiac surgery and angioplasty do not lower your risk of a later heart attack because they do not reduce the probability that these unidentified vulnerable plaques will rupture and create a clot.

Angioplasties, stent placements, and other cardiac surgeries treat symptoms, not the disease. Most people mistakenly think that periodic evaluations by cardiologists and radiologists are prudent steps in their efforts to avoid heart attacks (the idea being that they will get medical intervention at such time as a significant coronary blockage is detected). Unfortunately, you are at grave risk long before significant coronary blockage is detected.

Angioplasty itself (with or without stenting) damages the treated blood vessel, increasing inflammation and raising C-reactive protein, which in turn creates restenosis (reoccurrence of the narrowing due to the blood vessel wall swelling and scarring). This narrowing increases the risk of recurrent coronary events.[17]

Restenosis, which occurs in 30-50% of angioplasty-treated patients,[18] is more resistant to regression with nutritional approaches than native atherosclerosis. It represents a serious economic burden on society because treatment strategies now must include expensive approaches such as cutting-balloon angioplasty, rotational atherectomy, and brachytherapy. This is another important reason why you are far better off taking proven steps to prevent or reverse heart disease, before things get so bad that angioplasty is even considered.

Can you push cholesterol too low?

Occasionally, people ask if cholesterol can get too low. The short answer is no, but with a few caveats.

Typically, the people who promote the myth that low cholesterol levels are dangerous also promote the myth that animal-based diets, such as the Atkins diet, which is high in saturated fat and cholesterol, are safe. This nonsensical advice is not merely incorrect—it is dangerous. and it can lead to heart attack death for those who follow it.

There is no evidence that achieving low cholesterol levels through excellent health habits will increase your risk of heart disease or any other diseases. In fact, when a person eats and lives healthfully, low levels of cholesterol are a sign of good health.

Some people have naturally (genetically) low levels of cholesterol, regardless of what they eat. These low levels do not necessarily mean that anything is wrong with them healthwise (although it does not mean they are healthy, either). On the other hand, if your cholesterol is high, you are at increased risk for a heart attack and cancer and should take steps to achieve nutritional excellence immediately.

When it comes to preventing and reversing coronary artery disease, there may be no such thing as lowering total blood cholesterol levels too far. A study recently published in the journal *Circulation* found that the arteries in male patients with a total cholesterol level as low as 155 mg/dL benefited significantly from cholesterol-lowering medication.[19] Both regression of atherosclerosis and a dramatic reduction in heart attacks were seen in the group treated.

While some research in the past raised questions about the safety of very low cholesterol levels, no danger has been proven in larger, more dependable investigations. In fact, the latest research so strongly documents the effectiveness of substantial cholesterol lowering in saving lives, researchers now are debating the merits of aggressive cholesterol lowering even in young, seemingly healthy adults who show no overt signs of heart disease.

Low cholesterol controversy

In the 1980s, there was controversy about striving for lower, protective cholesterol levels after some studies noted that depression, suicide, hemorrhagic stroke, cancer, and death from other causes were higher in some groups with very low cholesterol. Larger, more recent investigations studying larger populations did not confirm these questionable findings.

When investigators looked more carefully at the individual characteristics of the studied populations, they were able to explain the earlier findings. What they found was that the studies did not account for the fact that bad health habits and poor health can cause low cholesterol in an unhealthy segment of the population.

For instance, cancer causes less cholesterol production in the liver. Consequently, low cholesterol may be associated with cancer. Researchers showed that cholesterol starts to fall up to eight years prior to a person dying of cancer, and that those with the greatest drop in cholesterol in a four-year period (without dietary improvements to lower cholesterol) were those most likely to develop cancer.[20] The low cholesterol did not cause the cancer; the cancer caused the low cholesterol. By contrast, individuals who work to lower cholesterol by avoiding saturated fats and eating a high-nutrient diet with lots of raw vegetables, cooked green vegetables, and beans have *healthfully* low cholesterol.

Heavy consumption of alcohol also causes liver damage that lowers cholesterol. So it should not come as a surprise that heavy drinkers (who are more likely to smoke cigarettes than the general population) have low blood cholesterol levels. Lung disease, alcoholism, certain types of cancers, and many other illnesses suppress appetite. People with these conditions eat less, causing their blood cholesterol levels to drop even further.

This issue of is complicated because the controversial studies evaluated individuals who were eating the modern American diet that is high in saturated fat and other components of animal products that raise cholesterol and low in plant-derived antioxidants, phytochemicals, and essential fatty acids that improve cholesterol ratios. Since you would expect people eating such a poor diet to have high cholesterol levels, the fact that these individuals had very low cholesterol levels indicates they actually may have had undetected chronic disease. In fact, when a person has a very low blood cholesterol level while on a diet high in saturated fat and cholesterol, the doctor should be alerted to watch for a hidden cancer; addiction to alcohol, cigarettes, or drugs; emotional disorder; or other disease.

Healthfully low cholesterol

In the United States, more than 40% of the population dies of heart attacks. Almost all American adults demonstrate significant coronary artery disease.[21] Young people are not immune to this plague. Autopsies of young trauma victims (who died before age thirty-five) revealed that 78% of them already had developed significant atherosclerosis.[22] If you eat the standard American diet (high in saturated fats and animal products), you will inevitably develop high cholesterol and the diseases that go with it.

Fortunately, there is no law that says you must eat like everybody else. The next time someone offers you a typical fat- and cholesterol-laden American-style meal, remember this:

The same massive Cornell-Oxford-China Study that discovered the low cholesterol levels and low heart attack rates (less than 5% of the population) in rural China where only very small amounts of animal foods are consumed discovered that heart disease rates were closely related to cholesterol levels. Where cholesterol levels were lowest, heart disease rates were lowest. These findings suggest that even small intakes of foods of animal origin are associated with significant increases in plasma cholesterol concentration, which in turn are associated with significant increases in heart disease mortality rates.[23]

You can achieve healthfully low cholesterol levels like those found in rural China through a steady diet of nutritional excellence, exercise, and appropriate supplementation as needed.

Heart Attack Prevention
that Actually Works

Now that you are fully aware of the serious ramifications of high cholesterol (such as, you die suddenly without warning) and the limitations of traditional medical care when it comes to protecting you, let's look at the almost unlimited protection you can give to yourself.

I am happy to tell you that both the symptoms of heart disease and the actual blockages and buildups that cause them easily melt away when you adopt my program of nutritional excellence. There is rarely a reason for anyone to risk complications of cardiac interventions and bypass surgeries when you can so safely implement an effective nutritional strategy. Instead of expensive and invasive medicine, most patients simply need doctors who are well versed enough to educate them and motivate them to make the necessary diet and lifestyle changes.

As I mentioned in the Introduction, during my fifteen years of practice, all of my cardiac patients who adopted the program of superior diet and appropriate supplementation improved or eliminated their heart conditions, and none subsequently suffered a heart attack. But you don't have to base your confidence on the successes of my patients alone. There is ample scientific research to give you all the confidence you need.

Compelling data from numerous population and intervention-al studies show that the combination of a natural, plant-based diet and aggressive lipid lowering will prevent, arrest, and even reverse heart disease. In fact, nutritional excellence is the *only* way that has ever been shown to naturally reduce the invisible, but potentially dangerous, plaque throughout your coronary arteries. More importantly, unlike surgery and angioplasty, the dietary approach not only heals your broken heart, it rejuvenates all your blood vessels and protects your entire body against heart attacks, strokes, pulmonary embolisms, venous thrombosis, peripheral vascular disease, and vascular dementia. It is your most valuable insurance policy to secure a longer life free of medical tragedy.

A look at a few important studies

Studies performed by Dean Ornish, M.D., of the University of California and other investigators have documented the effects of a low-fat, vegetarian diet on patients with heart disease, and found reversal of the condition occurred in the majority of patients. The reversal was modest, but nevertheless, no study previously showed diet could be so effective at preventing and reversing heart disease.[24]

Caldwell Esselstyn, Jr., M.D., of the Cleveland Clinic went a step farther and put together a program utilizing a vegetarian, plant-based diet with the addition of cholesterol-lowering medication in eighteen patients who had severe angiographically demonstrated coronary artery disease. All of these high-risk patients with advanced heart disease were noted to have no coronary events during the following twelve years, and on repeat angiogram, 70% were found to have regression of their disease, and none had progression.[25] When you consider that these patients had experienced 50 coronary events during the eight years before this study, you have to agree on the effectiveness of combining plant-based nutrition with cholesterol-lowering medication.

Dr. Esselstyn has tracked these patients for seventeen years, which is the longest ongoing research project of this kind, and not one of these people has had any further cardiac complaints or heart attacks. His study also has tracked the long-term results in six of his patients who did not want to adhere to the diet and returned to the standard care of their cardiologists. They experienced 13 new cardiac events during the first twelve years.

Dr. Esselstyn is a soft spoken, very caring human being, but when it comes to advising patients with heart disease, he plays hardball. He says, "Moderation kills. We must eliminate the lethal phrase 'this little bit won't hurt.'" In his medical practice, he only accepts patients who are totally committed to wiping out their disease and willing to do whatever it takes to stay well.

So how did this world-renowned surgeon at the Cleveland Clinic get so involved in the nutritional treatment of heart patients? Simply stated, he was frustrated that his patients were so sick and dying needlessly. He went looking for ways to keep his patients from needing surgery and suffering from an unnecessary premature death. What he found is the same thing I found—the combination of superior nutrition with a plant-based, vegetable-predominant diet and cholesterol-lowering therapy stops heart disease cold.

Additional protection

In recent years, I have made modifications to my nutritional program that have increased its effectiveness. I now use natural cholesterol-lowering therapies instead of drugs to eliminate the risk of drug side effects. My dietary program is richer in fiber and nutrients than the typical vegetarian and vegan diets, so my patients achieve spectacular reductions in cholesterol and body weight. They achieve predictable reversal of heart disease and protection from future cardiac-related death, and since nutritional excellence prevents and eliminates a host of other diseases, they also decrease their risk of death from all causes. Relieved of the fears of physical, emotional, and financial ruin, healthy people usually live more rewarding and pleasurable lives.

Does diet really matter that much?

It is entirely reasonable for you to ask why more people haven't heard that they can protect themselves so powerfully through nutritional excellence. Technically, people have heard about it. Newspapers have reported on the studies by Drs. Ornish and Esselstyn, and the China Study that I cited earlier (whose lead researcher, T. Colin Campbell, Ph.D., of Cornell University, is one of the biggest names in biochemistry) was called the "Grand Prix of Epidemiology" by *The New York Times*. But occasional newspaper reports cannot compete with daily TV reports about dubious studies (typically funded by food and drug corporations) and advertisements that reinforce people's bad eating habits and advertisers' profits. There is a lot more money to be made by selling hamburgers, heart medication, and bypass surgery than there is by telling people how to eat right.

Economic forces make it difficult for Americans to get sound scientific information about heart disease and the nutritional errors that cause it. For example, six of the eleven members, including the chairman, of the United States Department of Agriculture's Dietary Guidelines Committee in the year 2000 had financial ties to the meat, dairy, and egg industries. Not surprisingly, the foods these industries produce figure prominently in the government's recommended foods—despite the fact that these foods have documented links to increased health risks. Similar problems exist in the recommendations of nonprofit health organizations that receive funding from industry. Sadly, even the American Heart Association advocates a diet that has been shown to *increase* heart disease.[26]

Multiple dietary intervention trials have taken place testing diets suggested by the American Heart Association. Because these diets failed to show substantial benefits over the horrendous diets that most Americans eat, most medical authorities and physicians concluded that dietary modification was of little or no consequence. Little did they know that the diets suggested by the American Heart Association through the years have been nowhere near ideal. You can't expect to get major cardiac benefits by making minor changes to your diet.

Another reason why Americans know so little about how to eat right is that the media are always touting a new diet craze. It sometimes seems like there is a food-fad-of-the-month club promoting diets that range from the patently absurd (such as the Atkins, Zone, and Eat for Your Blood Type varieties) to some that are moderately beneficial, such as the Mediterranean diet and the Asian diet. The Mediterranean diet lowers heart disease risk about 30%, and the Asian diet lowers heart disease risk about 35%.

I am all in favor of lowering heart disease a little bit, but personally, I am not interested in making modest improvements when it comes to protecting myself and my family. Why take a few baby steps when with only the slightest bit more effort you will eliminate virtually 100% of the risk?

People deserve the truth.

Don't get me wrong. I am happy when people tweak their diets and reduce their risk of heart disease and other diseases a few percentage points. People have a right to eat (or smoke or drink, for that matter) however they want. What I want for people is for them to have full knowledge of what they are getting themselves into when they do these things.

I don't think it is right for doctors, dieticians, and health authorities to let people think that either a) diet doesn't matter, or b) some half-baked American Heart Association-type diet is going to protect them. I want people to have full and easy access to the fruits of modern nutritional science. Only then will people live long, healthful lives without strokes, heart attacks, cancer, or dementia. Every heart disease death is a tragedy, if for no other reason than because it simply did not have to happen.

The next time you hear about the latest and greatest new diet from exotic _____ (fill in the blank), remember that there are healthful aspects in the diets of almost every nationality and culture. There are unhealthful ones, too. And it is important to determine which is which. For example, people who are fond of the Mediterranean diet like to claim that it is healthful because it features generous servings of olive oil. If Mediterranean peoples are healthier than Americans (and with America's incredibly bad diet, it certainly is possible), it is more likely *in spite of* the olive oil consumption, rather than because of it.

As you will see in the recipe section, you can healthfully enjoy the best features of diets from around the world. The secret is that you need to understand what aspects of each cuisine account for the benefits, and which cause the problems!

A few case studies

Let's look at the outcomes of a few patients of mine who chose a program of dietary excellence rather than simply accepting the conventional medical approach.

John Palumbo

John first came to me as a patient in 1994, when he was age seventy-two. Prior to seeing me, he had reported experiencing pain in his chest and arms while exerting himself working in his backyard. Since even minimal activity caused discomfort, his physician gave him medications, including calcium channel blockers and nitroglycerin, to relieve his symptoms.

John also saw a cardiologist who performed a thallium stress test. The test indicated that John had ischemia, suggestive of multivessel coronary artery disease, so a cardiac catheterization (angiogram) was performed. The cardiac catheterization showed significant narrowing in his left and right main coronary arteries and 95% obstruction in both his left anterior descending artery and the opening of his marginal obtuse artery. Angioplasty was recommended, which he refused. His total cholesterol was 240 mg/dL, and his LDL cholesterol was 156 mg/dL. His fasting glucose was 98, and his creatinine was 1.5, suggestive of mild kidney damage. He weighed 171 at the time of his catheterization.

Upon becoming my patient, John followed my advice 100%. Within two months, he lost 14 pounds and had no further angina symptoms. He no longer needed any medications, and he was able to be active and to exercise without symptoms. After the first month, his total cholesterol was down to 168 mg/dL. When the cardiologist saw what great progress John was making using my aggressive dietary approach, he encouraged him to continue with the program and agreed with the cancellation of the angioplasty. In the ensuing months, while following my recommendations of what to eat and what cholesterol-lowering supplements to take, John's weight stabilized around 150 pounds, his LDL cholesterol came down to 84 mg/dL, and his creatinine dropped to 1.1 mg/dL.

John has been my patient for more than twelve years, and he has had no further heart problems. Now eighty-four, he works and plays aggressively and is experiencing excellent health.

Julia Spano

Julia Spano first became my patient in 2003, two months after reading my book *Eat to Live*. Julia not only lowered her cholesterol by changing her diet—she says she saved her life.

Prior to seeing me, Julia already had had three heart attacks—one in May 1999, one in February 2000, and a massive one in May 2000 that left her almost crippled. She was experiencing unstable angina (chest pains even at rest) and needed multiple medications to control her discomfort. She weighed 218 pounds before she read my book, but after two months of following my recommendations, she lost 32 pounds.

Within three months of following my nutritional advice, Julia's angina was gone. When she first came to me, she could not walk even one city block, but after the first six months, she was able to walk miles without difficulty. Her current weight is 135 pounds (after losing more than 80 pounds), and her LDL cholesterol is 61 mg/dL. Julia states, "You have given me my life back."

Of additional interest is the fact that Julia's other health challenge, polycythemia vera (a disease of increased red blood cells), has improved considerably as well, and she no longer requires ongoing treatment to lower her red blood cell count.

Bruce Fedora

I met Bruce when I was giving a lecture in San Francisco. He was never my patient, but he read my book, *Eat to Live,* and became a member of my website, DrFuhrman.com. After the lecture, he introduced himself and told me he had lost 80 pounds in the last year following my dietary program, and that his LDL cholesterol had dropped 80 points as well.

I was happy for Bruce and congratulated him. But success like that is not unusual. I have seen similar results in hundreds of patients. Then he told me an additional fact about his recovery, which was *very* unusual.

Bruce had undergone a Doppler ultrasound diagnostic test that indicated an 80% blockage of his carotid artery. He was told he was at high risk of a stroke and should undergo a carotid endarterectomy surgery to remove the blockage.

Bruce chose nutritional excellence instead, and in just one year, the 80% blockage disappeared.

When Bruce went back for a follow-up ultrasound at the end of the year, the ultrasonographer was amazed. He kept looking and looking to find some plaque, but it was gone.

The fortunate ones

Bruce, Julia, and John—and thousands of others—are fortunate to have found reliable scientific solutions to their life-threatening medical conditions. Not everyone is so lucky. Thousands of people suffer and die needlessly every day because their doctors offered them only drugs and surgery, rather than the powerful nutritional intervention that could have helped them.

I also feel fortunate. Helping people live happier, more healthful lives brings tremendous personal satisfaction. Nothing makes me happier than to receive heartfelt thanks from someone whom I have helped. (See letter on page 41.)

My fondest hope is that you decide to enjoy the benefits of my program of nutritional excellence. And once you have experienced the improved health and rejuvenation it brings, you also will want to tell family and friends about it. You will be living proof that:

- *There is a way to lower cholesterol and protect against heart attacks that is more effective than taking medications.*
- *You can accomplish it without the risks and high cost of drugs.*
- *By combining the safest and most healthful heart-protective approach to eating ever discovered with the most effective natural cholesterol-lowering supplements, you can achieve virtually total protection from heart disease.*
- *You can avoid angioplasty or coronary bypass surgery and actually reverse coronary disease that already has occurred.*

Dear Dr. Fuhrman,

On a whim, I searched the internet for a weight-loss diet to help with blood pressure. Your book *Eat to Live* happened to be the first one I found. I drove right to the bookstore, bought a copy, and read the whole book that afternoon. I could go on and on about my struggles, cravings, food addictions, and ultimate success, but I'll just let my "before" and "after" numbers speak for themselves.

Before starting your program, I weighed 190 pounds (I am 5'11"), my blood pressure was 130/72 (taking three medications to keep it down), and my total cholesterol was 192 (while taking one medicine).

After two months on your program, I went to visit my doctor. My weight was down to 165 pounds, my blood pressure was down to 124/86 (with no medication for over one month), and my total cholesterol was down to 132—triglycerides 45, LDL cholesterol 87, and HDL cholesterol 36.

My wife decided to do the program with me, and she has lost almost 30 pounds as well. You literally have saved our lives. We can't thank you enough.

Sincerely yours,

Shawn Flowers

When it comes to your health and your heart, do not be satisfied with modest improvements. I urge you to carefully study the critically important information in this book and make a decision to protect yourself and your family from the possibility of heartbreaking tragedy.

Chapter
4

Dietary Mistakes to Avoid

How healthful is *your* diet? Most people think their diets are reasonably healthful and that all they need to do is cut back on meat, desserts, and junk foods. In fact, most Americans' diets are overwhelmingly unhealthful. Remember, even if you buy all of your food in the health food store, it still is possible to be on a horrendously bad diet.

Let's be honest. Only those people who make a sincere and sustained effort to transform their diet and health are going to achieve the heart disease protection and recovery I am describing in this book. You are not going to be able to do it by making a few little temporary modifications to your diet. It will take significant, permanent changes. Sound daunting? It can seem like it at first. But thousands of other people have done it, so I know you can do it, too.

Before I describe the diet, menus, and foods I want you to eat, it is important for you to know some of the reasons why you need to stop eating the way you are now.

Killing ourselves with food

In the 20th century, the American diet shifted from one based on fresh, minimally processed vegetable foods to one based on animal products and highly refined, processed foods. As a result, Americans now consume far more fat, cholesterol, refined sugar, animal protein, sodium, and alcohol, and far fewer fiber and plant-derived nutrients than they need to maintain health. Obesity, diabetes, heart disease, and cancer have skyrocketed.

It is virtually impossible to eat the American diet without eventually developing a serious disease. Autopsy studies on adult Americans who die in car accidents show that over 95% of them have atherosclerotic heart disease. Heart disease and strokes kill over half of all Americans, and the only reason they don't kill the other half is because cancer or some other illness kills them first.

In the typical American diet, 40% of calories come from animal foods such as dairy, meat, eggs, and chicken, and 50% of calories come from processed foods such as pasta, bread, soda, oils, sugar, puffed cereals, pretzels, and other adulterated products. Only about 7% of calories come from unrefined plant foods—defined as fruits, vegetables, beans/legumes, and whole grains.

Facts about fats

Fat is one of the three macronutrients (along with protein and carbohydrate) that supplies calories to the body. Fats provide 9 calories per gram, more than twice the number provided by carbohydrates or protein.

Fat is necessary for the proper functioning of the body. Healthy skin and hair are maintained by fat. It helps in the absorption and transport through the bloodstream of the fat-soluble vitamins A,D,E, and K. Fats perform vital and valuable roles. For example, fats:

- *are a part of all cell membranes;*
- *make up part of the material that insulates nerves and increases the efficiency of nerve conduction;*

A glossary of fats

It is important that you know the differences between the types of fats, both because you need to make good food choices and because people talk about them (often inaccurately) all the time.

Saturated fats

Some naturally occurring fats are called "saturated" because all of the carbon atoms are single bonds. These fats are solid at room temperature and are generally recognized as a significant cause of both heart disease and cancer. Saturated fats are found mainly in meat, fowl, eggs, and dairy products. The foods with the most saturated fat are butter, cream, and cheese.

Saturated fat raises your LDL cholesterol level more than anything else in your diet. Eating too much saturated fat is the main reason for the high number of heart attacks seen in the Unites States and other countries.

Unsaturated fats

These fats are a mix of monounsaturated and polyunsaturated fat. You can lower your cholesterol by replacing saturated fats with unsaturated fats. Examples of unsaturated fats are the fats in nuts and seeds such as flaxseed, sunflower seeds, almonds, walnuts, cashews, macadamia nuts, and pistachio nuts, as well as those in avocados and olives. Keep in mind that while unsaturated fats can be considered "good" fats, eating excessive amounts may promote cancer and obesity.

Monounsaturated fats are fats with only one double bond in the carbon chain. They are liquid at room temperature. Monounsaturated fats are thought to be beneficial to health if they are used to replace dangerous saturated fats in the diet. Monounsaturated fats are found in avocados, olives, almonds, peanuts, and most other nuts.

Polyunsaturated fats are fats with more than one double bond in the carbon chain. Like monounsaturated fats, these natural fats are found in their natural state in raw seeds such as sesame and sun-

Continued on page 46

Glossary of Fats *(cont.)*

flower, as well as in corn and soybeans, and are essential for normal body development and function.

Hydrogenated fats (also called *trans fats*)

Hydrogenation is a process of adding hydrogen molecules to unsaturated fats, which makes plant oils that are liquid at room temperature solidify. (Margarine is an example of a product made by this process.) The hardening of the fat extends its shelf life so that the oil can be added to processed foods, such as crackers and cookies. Hydrogenated fats also can be used over and over again to fry potatoes, for example, in fast-food restaurants. While hydrogenation does not render the fat completely saturated, it creates trans-fatty acids, which act like saturated fats. These fats raise cholesterol, and increasing evidence is accumulating that demonstrates the harmful nature of these man-made fats and their relation to both cancer and heart disease. Avoid all foods whose ingredients contain hydrogenated and partially hydrogenated oils.

Cholesterol

Cholesterol is a waxy fat produced by the body and found in animal foods such as meat, fowl, dairy, and eggs. Eating cholesterol raises blood cholesterol, but, ironically, not as much as eating saturated fats and trans fats. The amount of cholesterol in plants is so negligible that you should consider them cholesterol-free.

Low density lipoprotein (LDL) cholesterol is the so-called "bad" cholesterol that promotes the plaque that leads to blockages and heart attacks. Thus, the more LDL cholesterol you have in your blood, the greater your risk of heart disease.

High density lipoprotein (HDL) cholesterol carries cholesterol back to the liver for removal from the body. It is called the "good" cholesterol because higher levels of HDL help keep fatty plaque from building up in the walls of the arteries. Individuals whose HDL cholesterol is low in relationship to their total cholesterol (a total cholesterol/HDL ratio above 4) are considered to have an exceptionally high risk of heart disease. Generally speaking, the higher your HDL cholesterol, the better. However, those with exceptionally low LDL cholesterol do not have to worry about their HDL cholesterol level. (You don't need as many garbage collectors when there is less garbage to clean up.)

Docosahexaenoic acid (DHA)

DHA is a long-chain omega-3 fat that is made by the body, but it also can be found in algae and fish, such as salmon and sardines. DHA is used in the production of anti-inflammatory mediators that inhibit abnormal immune function and prevent excessive blood clotting. DHA is not considered an essential fat because the body can manufacture sufficient amounts if adequate short-chain omega-3 fats (flax, walnuts, soybeans, and leafy green vegetables) are consumed. However, because of genetic differences in the enzyme activity, and because of excess consumption of omega-6 fats, many people who do not consume fish regularly are deficient in this important fat.

Arachidonic acid (AA)

AA is a long-chain omega-6 fat produced by the body, but also found in meat, fowl, dairy, and eggs. Byproducts formed as a result of consuming excessive amounts of this fatty acid have the potential to increase inflammation and cause disease. They can/may increase blood pressure, thrombosis, vasospasm, and allergic reaction and are linked to arthritis, depression, and other common illnesses.

Triglycerides

Triglycerides make up the largest proportion of fats (lipids) in your diet, adipose (fat) tissue, and blood. You store triglycerides in your fatty tissues and muscles as a source of energy, and gradually release and metabolize them between meals according to the energy needs of the body. Immediately after eating a fatty meal, triglycerides rise in the bloodstream. Consistently high blood-triglyceride levels are reflective of increased body fat stores, and high triglycerides promote and contribute to atherosclerosis in people with high cholesterol.

- *make up an integral part of certain hormones that regulate blood pressure, clotting, and inflammation;*
- *are the major component of brain tissue and are necessary for emotional well-being.*

Eating too much fat (just like eating too much carbohydrate and too much protein) can lead to weight gain and obesity, as well as coronary artery disease and other heart-related problems.

Just as certain vitamins and minerals are essential for health, certain fatty acids are essential; those that cannot be made by your body must be obtained from the food you eat. A heart-healthy diet should aim to include dietary fats in a balance with other nutrients to provide essential fatty acids to meet daily energy and other metabolic needs. Emphasis should be placed on minimizing or eliminating both saturated fats and trans fats.

Deadly saturated fats

Most researchers are coming to the same conclusions about saturated fat and heart disease—reducing or eliminating saturated fats must be high on every health-minded person's list of dietary priorities. Here is what the nutrition committee of the American Heart Association has concluded:

> *There is overwhelming evidence that reductions in saturated fat, dietary cholesterol, and weight offer the most effective dietary strategies for reducing total cholesterol, LDL cholesterol levels, and cardiovascular risk. Decreases in saturated fat should come at the expense of total fat [i.e., not be replaced with unsaturated fats] because there is no biological requirement for saturated fat.*[27]

All animal products contain unhealthful, unnecessary saturated fats, but cheese has the highest percentages of it, and even the lower-fat cheeses are high in artery-clogging saturated fat. Here are a few examples:

Cheese variety	Percentage of calories from fat	Percentage of fat that is saturated
Cream cheese	89%	63%
Gouda cheese	69%	64%
Cheddar cheese	74%	64%
Mozzarella cheese	69%	61%
Mozzarella cheese, part skim	56%	64%
Kraft Velveeta Spread	65%	66%
Kraft Velveeta Light	43%	67%
Ricotta, whole milk	68%	64%
Ricotta, part skim	51%	62%

Since eliminating saturated fat from your diet is one of the most effective ways to reduce cardiovascular risk, it makes sense to know how much of it is in various foods. That way, you know which ones to eliminate first. The chart above and the one on page 51 will help you get started.

Animal products and heart disease

Hundreds of respected scientific studies have shown that as animal products increase in a population's diet, cholesterol levels soar, and the occurrence of heart disease increases proportionally with the increase in animal product intake.[28] These research studies show that saturated fat is the element of the modern diet most closely associated with high cholesterol and premature death from heart attacks.[29]

Although saturated fat is the most heart disease-promoting substance in animal products, it is not the only problem. Animal protein raises cholesterol, too. Those who eliminate red meat from their diets and replace it with chicken and fish do not see substantial changes in their cholesterol levels or a profound reduction in cardiac events.[30]

If you are looking for maximum protection from heart disease, 90-100% of the calories in your diet must come from unrefined plant foods. You can include very small amounts of animal products, but if you have more than one or two servings per week, you are not going to see the huge drop in cholesterol level and heart disease risk observed in those eating a truly plant-based diet. One serving of nonpolluted fish and one serving of white meat fowl per week is the absolute most you should eat if you are looking for maximal protection against heart disease.

In recent years, there has been a torrent of books touting the benefits of high-protein diets for weight loss. These are very popular because they appeal to the huge market of people who are addicted to high-fat, nutrient-inadequate animal foods. Aside from the fact that these scientifically indefensible diets do not result in permanent weight loss, they are extremely dangerous. All animal products are severely deficient in fiber, phytochemicals, and anti-oxidants, and they contain too much saturated fat, cholesterol, and arachidonic acid.

Let me repeat. Research shows—without question—that as animal product consumption goes up in a country or population group, so do heart attacks. As animal product consumption goes down, so do heart attacks. You cannot prevent or reverse heart disease while continuing to consume significant amounts of animal foods. In countries where few refined foods were eaten and animal products accounted for less than 10% of the calories consumed (such as Mozambique, the Fiji Islands, and Guatemala prior to the 1970s), the populations were virtually free from heart disease. But as American-style fast foods have been adopted in those countries, heart disease has quickly followed.

Saturated fat content of common foods[31]

Common foods	Portion size	Grams of saturated fat
Cheddar cheese	(4 oz.)	24
American processed cheese	(4 oz.)	24
Ricotta cheese	(1 cup)	20
Swiss cheese	(4 oz.)	20
Chocolate candy, semisweet	(4 oz.)	20
Cheeseburger	(large double patty)	18
T-bone steak	(6 oz.)	18
Braised lamb	(6 oz.)	16
Pork shoulder	(6 oz.)	14.5
Butter	(2 Tbsp.)	14
Mozzarella, part skim	(4 oz.)	12
Ricotta cheese, part skim	(one cup)	12
Ground beef, lean	(6 oz.)	11
Vanilla ice cream	(one cup)	10
Chicken fillet sandwich	(4 oz.)	9
Chicken thigh, no skin	(6 oz.)	5
Whole milk, 3.3% fat	(one cup)	5
Plain yogurt	(1 cup)	5
Two eggs	medium-sized	4
Chicken breast	(6 oz.)	3
Salmon	(6 oz.)	3
2% milk	(one cup)	3
Tuna	(6 oz.)	2.6
Flounder	(6 oz.)	0.6
Sole	(6 oz.)	0.6
Fruits		negligible
Vegetables		negligible
Beans/legumes		negligible

Author's note: There is no biological requirement for saturated fat.

Refined foods and increased disease

Refined grain products such as white bread, pasta, bagels, white rice, most breakfast cereals, and other denatured and processed grains are almost as nutrient-deficient as sugar. The nutritional value of these "foods" is very low compared with healthful, unrefined foods, which are rich in fiber and anticancer nutrients.

In a six-year study of 65,000 women, the women with diets high in refined carbohydrates from white bread, white rice, and pasta had two and one-half times the incidence of Type II diabetes, compared with those who ate high-fiber foods, such as vegetables, beans/legumes, whole grains, and fresh fruit.[32] Diabetes is the fourth leading cause of death by disease in America, and the number of people developing diabetes is soaring. White flour, other refined grains such as sweetened breakfast cereals, soft drinks, other sweets, and even fruit juices are weight-promoting and not only lead to diabetes, but can raise triglycerides and cholesterol levels, increasing heart attack risk.

Processed foods commonly include refined sweets such as sugar, honey, corn syrup, molasses, and corn sweeteners that contain no fiber and only insignificant amounts of nutrients per calorie. Numerous studies offer evidence that the consumption of white-flour products and sweets such as these can be a significant cause of obesity, diabetes, heart disease, and even cancer.[33]

Each time you eat processed foods, you miss out not only on important known nutrients and phytonutrients, but also on all of the yet undiscovered phytonutrients. For instance, when the outer portion of the wheat kernel is removed to make flour "white," trace minerals, phytoestrogens, lignins, phytic acid, indoles, phenolic compounds, and other phytochemicals (as well as 90% of the fiber and vitamin E) are removed with it. A full complement of micronutrients, both known and unknown, is needed to ward off disease.

Additionally, when you eat baked goods, cold breakfast cereals, pretzels, and other snack foods, you are ingesting heart disease-promoting trans fats and a high dose of acrylamides. Acrylamides are toxic, cancer-promoting compounds produced when foods are baked or fried at high temperatures. Chips, pretzels, cold breakfast cereals, roasted soy nuts, browned foods, crusted foods, and fried foods contain high levels of these toxic compounds that are formed when carbohydrates are exposed to high, dry heat. These harmful compounds are not formed when foods are water-cooked, such as when you steam vegetables or make soups.

Refined or processed foods often include refined oils. All oils are nutrient-poor and pack a whopping 120 calories per tablespoon. The process of extracting oils from plants leaves behind all of the fiber and most of the nutrients and antioxidants that were in the original food. When you eat these high-calorie, nutrient-poor oils instead of comparable amounts (calorie-wise) of whole plant foods, you dramatically reduce the nutrients and antioxidants in your overall diet.

Ruining salads with oily dressings

Vegetables and salads are high in nutrients and low in calories. However, if you cover these wonderful foods with a few tablespoons of a high-fat, high-calorie, oil-based dressing, you turn what could have been a healthful meal into a low-nutrient (calorie-wise), weight-promoting meal. Americans consume an average of three tablespoons of oil each day, adding an extra 360 calories to their daily intake. To maximally protect against and reverse heart disease, you need to reach the ideal weight for your body type.

Refined vegetable oils are an improvement over butter and margarine, but they still promote weight gain, and therefore are not heart disease-protective.

I know that food editors like to tout olive oil and certain other oils as "health" foods, but they aren't. All oils are processed, and are far from whole, "natural" foods. Use oils sparingly or not at all. Certainly, do not have more than one teaspoon per day.

Whole foods best

The whole foods that oils come from always contain more nutrients and have a higher nutrient-to-calorie ratio than the extracted oils. For example, flaxseed oil, like other oils, contains 120 calories per tablespoon. By contrast, ground flaxseed contains only 30 calories per tablespoon and contains more lignins, flavonoids, beneficial fibers, sterols, and a host of other beneficial substances. Excessive amounts of oil are not favorable, and even too much of the beneficial oil in flax is linked to higher rates of prostate cancer.[34] Eat the food, not the extracted oil.

As an alternative to oil, you can make great tasting salad dressings from avocados and raw nuts and seeds, such as flax, walnuts, pecans, cashews, sunflower seeds, sesame seeds, and pistachios. It is easy to make delicious, heart-healthy, nutrient-rich dressings by blending fresh fruit, a small amount of ground or whole nuts or seeds, and one of the great tasting fruit-flavored vinegars available from my website.

Many of my personal favorite dressing recipes are included in Chapter 7. They are more tasty and more healthful than the salty, oil-laden, commercially made salad dressings. Once you learn to make these tasty dressings (and start inventing your own), you will relish your big salads like never before.

Traditionally, nuts have been perceived as unhealthful because of their high fat content. However, recent accumulative evidence suggests that the regular consumption of nuts is remarkably protective against heart disease and cancer (which I describe in more detail in Chapter 6).

When you consume your fats as nutrient-rich whole foods—such as nuts, seeds, and avocados—instead of nutrient-poor extracted oils, you get lignins, flavonoids, and other valuable nutrients that support excellent health.

Salt and stroke risk

Salt is linked to hypertension and increased cardiovascular disease. By no stretch of the imagination can salt be considered a healthful food. All types of salt—sea salt, Celtic salt, and other so-called "natural" salts—carry the same dangerous risks as ordinary salt. The miniscule amount of extra minerals contained in these higher priced salts is insignificant compared to the minerals found in food, and their presence in no way makes these salts less harmful.

In addition to the usual problems associated with salt consumption, it is important to note that under certain otherwise heart-healthy conditions, a high-salt diet can increase your risk of a less common type of stroke, called hemorrhagic stroke.

There are two types of strokes: *embolic* strokes (the most common type) and *hemorrhagic* strokes (which occur only one-tenth as often). High cholesterol is a risk factor for embolic stroke. Low cholesterol is normally an indication of protection against stroke. But when undermined by a high-salt diet, it can become a risk factor for hemorrhagic stroke.

A hemorrhagic stroke occurs when a fragile blood vessel in the brain ruptures, usually as a result of years and years of high blood pressure, which eventually weakens the vessel. Oddly enough, the same unhealthful diet that fosters the atherosclerotic (plaque-building) process that can lead to embolic stroke actually may prevent hemorrhagic strokes (by thickening, and thereby strengthening, what would otherwise be fragile blood vessels in the brain).

Admittedly, compared to embolic strokes, hemorrhagic strokes account for a very small percentage of the deaths in modern countries. However, a number of studies in Japan (where a high-salt diet has made stroke a leading cause of death) and elsewhere have illustrated that low serum cholesterol associated with low consumption of animal products increases the risk of hemorrhagic stroke.[35]

The message is clear. A healthful, low-saturated-fat, predominantly vegetarian diet will markedly reduce risk for coronary heart disease, diabetes, and many common cancers. However, to avoid the risk of hemorrhagic stroke, vegans and others on diets with few animal products must avoid high salt intake. If you consume salt, it is inevitable that your blood pressure will increase over time, putting the fragile blood vessels in your brain at risk of hemorrhagic stroke. Of course, excess sodium increases heart attacks and strokes in all types of diets, and the greatest risk of stroke occurs if you eat the typical American diet. But it is worth knowing the dangers of ruining an otherwise heart-healthy approach to diet by adding high salt intake.

Needless to say, I do not advocate adding salt to any foods.

By contrast, very few vegan, vegetarian, or other health-minded diets warn against salt consumption, and some openly advocate it (as long as it is salt with a fancy name). As a result, salt is in almost every so-called "health food." Almost all of the soy-based meat analogues and many other health food store (vegan) products are exceptionally high in sodium, as are many other processed and prepared vegetarian, vegan, and macrobiotic foods. (And, virtually all standard American packaged foods are loaded with it.)

Safe, healthful diet

Rest assured, there is no need to fear a hemorrhagic stroke if you do not eat salt and do not have high blood pressure. Natural foods contain all the sodium you need; you don't need extra sodium. The natural, plant-based diet I recommend in this book will maintain sodium intake below 1,000 mg per day. At that level, there is no increased risk of hemorrhagic stroke. It is well established that Third World countries that do not salt their food are virtually immune to hypertension, and strokes are not observed in rural populations that eat natural foods and do not use salt in their diets.

Special Note to Young People

Vegans, whether they eat high-salt diets or not, typically do not experience fatal heart attacks when they are relatively young. But because they tend to live longer, vegans who eat high-salt diets (therefore being more likely to develop hypertension) increase their risk of hemorrhagic stroke later in life because their hypertension has had more years to weaken the fragile blood vessels in the brain.

Even if you don't have high blood pressure now, high salt intake will inevitably take its toll. Unfortunately, by the time that happens, it can be difficult to return your blood pressure to normal, even if the salt intake is eliminated.

Eliminate salt from your diet today!

Chapter

5

A Heart-Protective Diet

The heart-protective dietary recommendations in this book are distilled from my book *Eat to Live: The Revolutionary Formula for Fast and Sustained Weight Loss. Eat to Live* is an exhaustive treatise on the healthiest way for people to achieve their ideal weight that is supported by more than 1,000 scientific references. Once you master the cholesterol-specific dietary principles presented in this book, I encourage you to read *Eat to Live,* if for no other reason than it has an extensive recipe section, and it will help you to lose weight.

A recent investigative review by T.C. Campbell, Ph.D., of Cornell University and Barbara Sarter, Ph.D., of the University of Southern California Medical Center found that those following the *Eat to Live* program for two years had the most successful sustained weight loss ever recorded by any dietary intervention in medical history. Achieving your ideal weight is a prerequisite for the highest levels of health.

The guiding concept for establishing a heart-protective diet is as follows:

$$H = N/C$$

(Health = Nutrients divided by Calories)

I call $H = N/C$ the health equation. Put simply, the healthfulness of both the individual foods you eat and your overall diet can be determined by looking at the relationship of nutrients to calories. Foods high in nutrients and low in calories (vegetables) are the best; foods high in calories and low in nutrients (animal products and highly processed foods) are the worst. Since your risk of heart disease and cancer can be predicted by the nutrient-per-calorie density of your diet over your lifetime, it makes sense to adopt a high nutrient-per-calorie diet. It is the absolute best way to maximize your health.

Most readers of this book are looking for protection against heart disease. I am happy to report that the same dietary habits that make you heart attack-proof also protect you against a host of other diseases (and help you lose weight). The consumption of high-calorie, nutrient-deficient foods (also called "empty calorie" foods) is spreading like an epidemic all over the globe. Not surprisingly, heart disease, obesity, and diabetes are becoming the leading causes of death almost everywhere. There is a strong link between the consumption of low-nutrient foods and the devastating heart disease, strokes, and cancers that cause 85% of all deaths in America.

High-nutrient foods

Most people (even many doctors) are shocked to learn that animal products are extremely nutrient-deficient compared with vegetables. The meat and dairy industries have spent billions of dollars on advertising and lobbying campaigns that promote their products as superior foods, packed with important nutrients that are *necessary* for health. The opposite is closer to the truth. The most important nutrients (fiber, vitamins, minerals, phytonutrients, and antioxidants) are low or nonexistent in animal products. Animal products are perfect examples of high-calorie, low-nutrient foods, and because they pack such a huge number of calories into a small portion of food, it is very easy to overeat them. By contrast, when you get your calories from high-nutrient plant foods, you get a huge number of nutrients, phytonutrients, antioxidants, and plenty of protein, plus you can eat as much as you want without worrying about overeating.

The chart below shows how poorly meat compares in nutrient content with three common green vegetables.

Nutrients per 100-calorie portions of selected foods[36]

	Sirloin steak	Broccoli	Romaine lettuce	Kale
Protein	5.4 gm	11.2 gm	7.5 gm	11 gm
Calcium	2.4 mg	322 mg	374 mg	470 mg
Iron	.7 mg	3.5 mg	7.7 mg	5.8 mg
Magnesium	5 mg	74.5 mg	60.5 mg	97 mg
Potassium	88 mg	1084 mg	1452 mg	836 mg
Fiber	0	4.7 g	4 g	3.4 g
Folate	3 mcg	257 mcg	969 mcg	60 mcg
B2	.04 mg	.71 mg	.45 mg	.32 mg
Niacin	1.1 mg	2.8 mg	2.2 mg	2.1 mg
Zinc	1.2 mg	1.04 mg	1.2 mg	.55 mg
Vitamin C	0	350 mg	100 mg	329 mg
Vitamin A	24 IU	7750 IU	10,450 IU	23,407 IU
Vitamin E	0	26 IU	32 IU	34 IU
Cholesterol	55 mg	0	0	0
Saturated fat	1.7 gm	0	0	0
Phytochemicals	0	Very high	Very high	Very high
Antioxidants	0	Very high	Very high	Very high
Weight	24 gm (.84 oz)	307 gm (10.6 oz)	550 gm (19 oz)	266 gm (9.2 oz)

Superiority of plant foods

The nutrient-density superiority of green vegetables compared with meat is an important fact to understand. Many people mistakenly think that saturated fat is the reason why animal products, such as milk, cheese, butter, meat, and chicken, are linked so closely with illness and premature death in America. This leads to the notion of trying to commercially manufacture or genetically engineer low-fat or no-fat versions of these "foods." But reducing or eliminating high-fat foods from your diet is only beneficial if you replace them with high-nutrient plant foods.

Let's take a look at some of the reasons why plant foods are so protective and essential for human health. Prior to seeing the chart on page 61, did you know that green vegetables contain more protein per calorie than meat? That fact may be easier to digest and assimilate if you recall that the largest land animals—elephants, gorillas, rhinoceroses, hippopotamuses, and giraffes—eat diets made up predominantly of green vegetation. Grass, leaves, and other plant foods must pack an incredible protein punch because these huge animals obviously are getting enough protein.

Green vegetables are loaded with powerful nutrients and phytochemicals that fuel your immune system and your internal self-repair mechanisms. Without an abundant supply of green vegetables, you are forced to function without your full protective armor against disease.

Numerous scientific investigations have shown one category of food to have a strong, positive association with increased longevity in humans—raw, leafy green vegetables. Leafy greens, such as the romaine lettuce, kale, collards, Swiss chard, and spinach that you put in salads, are the most healthful foods you can eat. And since they are low in calories, they help you lose weight. (In fact, as you adopt the *Eat to Live* approach, you will need to greatly *increase* the portion sizes you eat because the foods that are the highest in nutrient density are the lowest in calories.) In a review of 206 human epidemiological studies, green vegetables showed the strongest protective effect against cancer compared with all other beneficial foods. Unfortunately, only 1 in 500 Americans consumes enough calories from vegetables to assure this defense.

I tell my patients to put a big sign on their refrigerator to remind themselves that:

THE SALAD IS THE MAIN DISH!

High green vegetable consumption is associated with powerful protection against both heart attack and cancer. That is why the cornerstone of your new, heart-protective diet is to eat as many raw and steamed green vegetables as you can. The more of these "super foods" you eat, the higher the nutrient density of your diet will be. Most vegetables are higher in nutrient density than any other foods. Many vegetables contain more protein per calorie than meat, and many have more calcium per calorie than milk. For example, romaine lettuce is a rich powerhouse containing hundreds of cancer-fighting phytonutrients that gets 50% of its calories from protein and 18% of its calories from unsaturated fat. Kale is even higher in protein and has over 20% more calcium per calorie than milk.

If you eat like most Americans, or even if you follow the USDA's food pyramid recommendations precisely (6-11 servings of bread, rice, and pasta made from refined grains and 4-6 servings of dairy, meat, poultry, or fish), you are eating a diet high in calories and dangerously low in nutrients, phytochemicals, antioxidants, and vitamins. Eating like that will leave you overfed and undernourished, and you will have the precise nutritional profile that leads to heart disease, cancer, and diabetes.

Documented success

Unlike the seemingly never ending parade of fad diets, and even the American Heart Association's recommended low-fat diet, my plant-based, high-nutrient-per-calorie diet has shown dramatic, documented success at lowering cholesterol. The chart below shows the cholesterol-lowering effect, over a 6-week time period, of various dietary interventions as documented in published medical journal articles.[37]

6-week cholesterol-lowering effect of various intervention methods	*Percentage of LDL decrease*
High-protein/Atkins-type[38]	No significant change
High-olive oil/Mediterranean[39]	No significant change
American Heart Association/standard low-fat advice[40]	6%
Low-fat vegetarian[41]	16%
Cholesterol-lowering statin medications[42]	26%
Eat to Live/Fuhrman-type[43]	33%

The *Eat to Live* approach is the only dietary intervention ever shown in medical studies to lower cholesterol more effectively than cholesterol-lowering medication, a fact that was reported in the medical journal *Metabolism* in 2001. All other dietary interventions have been relatively ineffective at lowering cholesterol. As you can see from the chart (above), the low-fat vegetarian diet lowered LDL cholesterol 16%, but it raised triglycerides 18.7%, and the LDL/HDL ratio remained unchanged (reflecting only minimal overall improvement). The *Eat to Live* results were far better. LDL cholesterol was lowered significantly, and there were no unfavorable impacts on HDL cholesterol or triglycerides (reflecting sizable reduction of cardiac risk factors).

The results of medical studies referenced in the chart corroborate the results achieved in my clinical practice with thousands of patients utilizing the *Eat to Live* approach, and show the superior ability of nutritional excellence to lower cholesterol and prevent cardiac deaths. Hopefully, the advantages of nutritional intervention soon will become more widely appreciated by medical authorities, physicians, and the population at large.

Plant-based vs. starch-based

Many people think that all vegan and vegetarian diets are alike, with the bulk of calories coming from whole grains and highly processed foods such as soy cheese and various meat and dairy substitutes (or actual dairy products, in the case of vegetarians). My *Eat to Live* program is entirely different because the emphasis is on vegetables. The chart below points out the major differences.

Eat to Live Program	Starch-Based Vegan Diet
1. low-carbohydrate diet with an emphasis on colorful vegetables, beans, and mushrooms	1. high-carbohydrate diet with an emphasis on rice, potatoes, bread, and pasta
2. generous servings of fruits	2. less fruit
3. raw, unsalted nuts (for a substantial caloric contribution)	3. fewer nuts
4. minimal or no animal products	4. no animal products
5. no processed foods	5. some processed foods
6. higher in fiber	6. lower in fiber
7. higher nutrient levels	7. lower nutrient levels
8. lower in sodium	8. higher in sodium
9. higher in omega-3 fats	9. lower in omega-3 fats

While vegan and vegetarian diets are usually a step in the direction of health (primarily as a result of limiting or eliminating animal products), they typically fall short when it comes to nutrient-per-calorie density.

Vegetables are far more nutrient-per-calorie dense than grains and starches (and oils). In addition to the superior nutritional benefits it provides, eating lots of vegetables helps ensure that you do not consume more calories than you actually need. Remember, the only thing that has been shown to significantly extend life span (documented in hundreds of scientific studies) is reducing caloric consumption while still consuming adequate nutrients. It should be obvious that the only way to do this is to eat a high-nutrient diet with a highly positive H=N/C ratio. The *Eat to Live* program supplies all of the vitamins, minerals, fiber, antioxidants, bioflavonoids, and phytochemicals necessary for normal body functioning without requiring you to eat any excess calories.

Weight and health

If you don't think excess weight is a national (and increasingly international) problem, consider this: Americans spend $40 billion each year on diets and reducing programs. As you will see, one delightful side effect of eating a genuinely healthful diet is that you will reach your ideal weight without counting calories or measuring portions. When you learn which foods are best, you can eat as much of them as you desire.

Getting thinner is extremely important to maximally lower your cholesterol and protect yourself from heart disease and cancer. You can't expect to get the fat out of your heart until you get the fat off of your waist. Excess weight increases your LDL cholesterol level. If you are overweight and have a high LDL cholesterol level, losing weight will help lower it. Weight loss also helps to lower triglycerides and raise HDL cholesterol. Regular exercise also lowers LDL cholesterol and raises HDL cholesterol, making it a vital component of your cardiac-health program. In fact, regular exercise and high-nutrient diet are more important for cardiac health than taking either medicine or nutritional supplements.

If your diet does not consist primarily of colorful, nutrient-rich plant foods, toxic cellular wastes will accumulate. This toxic accumulation leaves you more susceptible to disease and contributes to premature aging. One of the reasons that the *Eat to Live* approach is so effective at lowering cholesterol, improving health, and losing weight is that it requires you to eat a large quantity of healthful food, which in turn provides all of the nutrients and phytochemicals necessary to fuel cellular detoxification and repair.

Cellular toxicity can turn you into a "food addict," craving more food and calories than your body actually needs. When your intake of micronutrients is consistently low, cellular toxicity builds up, creating an internal environment that triggers food cravings and sensations of illness (headaches, weakness, abdominal spasm and fluttering, mental confusion, and more) whenever you go without food for a few hours. You become like a heroin, nicotine, or caffeine addict who needs a regular fix to prevent uncomfortable withdrawal symptoms. People typically mistake these withdrawal symptoms for hunger and become addicted to frequent eating (and overeating) just to make the discomfort go away. Withdrawal symptoms are not a call from your body for food, they are a sign that your body is struggling in its efforts to effectively deal with (detoxify) the excess waste products that have built up in your tissues.

Eat to Live is the only dietary approach that recognizes "toxic hunger" as a cause of obesity, and the only way to break free from its debilitating grasp is to elevate the nutrient-per-calorie density of your diet. As long as your diet is made up primarily of low-nutrient foods (such as bread, pasta, cold cereals, refined carbohydrates, oil, and animal products), it will be impossible to lose weight healthfully. In fact, a lifetime of eating typical "American" food almost guarantees that you will become overweight or obese, especially if you don't exercise regularly.

Over time, eating large amounts of high-nutrient food turns off the toxic hunger and eliminates your desire for frequent eating (and overeating). When you ingest an adequate level of nutrients, your brain receives the appropriate signals that you have met your nutritional needs, and the cravings and toxic hunger diminish.

Eliminating toxic hunger almost always eliminates the need to ever diet again. As your taste buds and food preferences change, your enjoyment of healthful meals will increase, and your weight will decrease. As you get closer to your ideal weight, weight loss gradually slows down and eventually stops. Your body is a very intelligent "machine." When you eat correctly, it will achieve its ideal weight effortlessly.

Lately, there has been a lot of talk about the role our genes play in the development of diseases. While this makes for interesting discussions at cocktail parties, understand that even if you have a genetic predisposition to develop a particular condition, you are not likely to develop it unless you commit a great number of nutritional errors (such as eating the standard American diet). If you avoid the high-calorie, low-nutrient foods that most people eat, and consume a diet that is made up almost exclusively of nutrient-dense foods,

Why most diet programs fail

The traditional approach to dieting—cutting calories—fails over 90% of the time. When you cut back on your food intake, food cravings arise, along with uncomfortable symptoms related to cellular toxicity from eating a nutrient-poor diet. If you eat often enough to quell the toxic hunger (withdrawal symptoms)—your weight comes right back. When you eat properly, toxic hunger gradually disappears, and your excess weight simply melts away.

Diets also fail because most people don't know that they are overweight because of *what* they eat, not because of *how much* they eat. It is a myth that we get heavy because we consume a high volume of food. In fact, eating a high volume of foods high in antioxidants and phytochemicals is the only way to achieve permanent, healthful weight loss. For a weight-loss program to be successful, it must involve dietary changes that you can live with for the rest of your life. Eating like a bird might help you slip into a smaller dress size for a couple of months, but eventually your body is going to cry out for nutrients. At that point, there will be great temptation to break down and soothe the pain with the same unhealthful foods that put the weight on in the first place. When news of the next party, wedding, boy/girlfriend, or _____ (fill in the blank) appears on the horizon, the cycle will begin all over again.

One of the difficulties of trying to adopt a program of nutritional excellence is the fact that almost no one knows what we are supposed to eat. Lots of otherwise savvy people think high-calorie, low-nutrient foods like pasta, chicken, and olive oil are healthful. After reading this book, you'll know better.

Don't treat your excess weight lightly. If the only negative consequences of being overweight were rude stares and comments from insensitive people, I'd say eat, drink, and be merry. But insensitivity is the least of your worries if you are overweight. The diet of high-fat, low-nutrient animal foods and highly refined carbohydrates that causes the excess weight in the first place puts you at terrible risk for diseases like cancer, heart disease, diabetes, and dementia.

you can practically disease-proof yourself. When you consistently eat healthfully, you enhance your body's ability to defend against illness and keep any genetic weaknesses at bay.

Quick weight loss

You will be happy to know that your body drops its excess weight relatively quickly when you adopt the *Eat to Live* program. And if you permanently adopt the program, the weight loss will be permanent. By mastering the concepts presented in this book, you will become an expert at eating healthfully in most circumstances. You may need a little help and support at first (I encourage you to read *Eat to Live* and to take advantage of the online knowledge base and membership services at DrFuhrman.com), but the more you learn, the easier it will be to achieve nutritional excellence. In this program, knowledge and understanding motivate change, not willpower or deprivation.

Eat to Live is marketed as a weight-loss book because the program it describes virtually guarantees successful weight loss. Even those with metabolic hindrance to weight loss will lose weight easily. But the benefits of this approach go far beyond weight loss. By achieving nutritional excellence, you will decrease your risk of heart disease and cancer dramatically.

Dear Dr. Fuhrman,

I am 41 years old and have had cholesterol levels in the low 200s for most of my adult life. My father died at the age of 40 (I had just turned 5) of a massive heart attack, and my mother has had claudication in her legs. With such a family history, I have been afraid that I also would suffer a premature death and leave my husband and 6-year-old son well before it was time.

About a week after I started your plan, I had a cholesterol test done. My total cholesterol was 212. I had another test done two weeks later and was delighted to learn that it had dropped to 175 (LDL 113; HDL 48; triglycerides 72). The nurse was very impressed by the 37-point drop in just two weeks and wanted to know how I did it. Of course, I still have a ways to go. I haven't lost all of the weight I need to lose (currently 162 at 5'7" after starting out at 175), but I am very pleased and motivated to continue with the program. In fact, I just joined your online membership this week.

I love eating the *Eat to Live* way, and it has not been too hard of a switch, especially since the food cravings I'd been plagued with for several years have vanished.

I am sure that you get letters like this all the time, but I wanted to let you know how grateful I am. I am no longer haunted by the fear that history will repeat itself, and that my young son will lose me to a heart attack like I lost my father.

Sincerely,

Sharon Herman

Chapter 6

Dietary Guidelines for Lowering Cholesterol

T he *Eat to Live* dietary program is scientifically proven to lower cholesterol and promote heart health. And in addition to heart attack prevention, using this approach will help you lose weight, live longer, and avoid other debilitating diseases (such as cancer, diabetes, and dementia) as well. Armed with your new knowledge about nutrition, you will be able to achieve dietary transformation relatively effortlessly. Plus, as you build up your own personal experiences, you will become more of an expert in matters of diet and health than many people in the health field.

In this chapter, I describe the ten most important guidelines for lowering cholesterol (eleven if you count the admonition not to eat salt). Put these guidelines into practice on a daily basis, and you will be well on your way to disease-proofing yourself and looking ahead to years of joyful, vibrant health. But remember, while the *Eat to Live* approach is knowledge-based (rather than denial- or self discipline-based), you need more than knowledge—you need to put your knowledge into practice.

When I made nutrition my medical specialty, I focused my attention on individuals who were looking for dietary intervention as a means of reversing their medical conditions to recover their health, thoughtful individuals who could understand the risks inherent in traditional medical care and who wanted to avoid a lifetime of medication and invasive surgeries. This decision has proven to be magnificently rewarding. When patients make a commitment to superior health through nutritional excellence, they can reduce and eventually stop their dependency on medications for high blood pressure, high cholesterol, diabetes, and a host of other conditions. Spectacular heart disease reversals have become the norm, not the exception.

I urge you to adopt the *Eat to Live* program today and begin the journey to lowered cholesterol and permanent heart health.

Cholesterol-Lowering Guidelines

1. *My recommended dietary program is vegetable-based, not grain-based.* Eat as many fresh and frozen vegetables as you can. Frozen vegetables are very nutrient dense. They are harvested, steamed, and frozen on the same day, locking in the nutrients. Feel free to throw a box of frozen artichoke hearts, asparagus, or peas on your salad whenever you'd like. You also can add as much eggplant, onions, and mushrooms as you desire. Eggplant and beans, mushrooms and beans, and greens and beans each make high-nutrient, high-fiber, low-calorie main dishes. Try all of the combinations and experiment with the many delicious ways to flavor them.

2. *Eat as many raw vegetables as possible.* Eat unlimited quantities of raw vegetables, including raw starches such as carrots. Raw foods fill you up and encourage weight loss. Since it is impossible to overeat salad and lettuce, you can eat as much of them as you want. I tell many of my patients to try to eat at least one entire head of romaine lettuce each day. Every lunch and every din-

ner should begin with a salad and/or some other raw vegetables.

As a variation, you can drink a glass of freshly squeezed raw vegetable juice in addition to the salad at one of your meals. Try juicing various combinations of carrots and apples, carrots and cucumbers, and tomatoes and beets. It is always good to add some greens to the juice. In fact, you can make a particularly healthful dish by simply blending your salad. (Blend salad vegetables and some fresh juice or water in a blender to make a green smoothie.) Raw salad greens are "wonder foods" for your health, and when you blend them into a smoothie, you get more of their powerful nutrients. (The blades of the blender break down the cell walls, dramatically increasing the bioavailability of the nutrients.)

My wife and I eat blended salads frequently. We frequently take baby romaine lettuce and blend it with a banana, an apple, and a couple of dates. Blended salads enable us to consume 3-4 ounces of raw leafy greens quickly and easily and to glean their powerful health effects. Blended salads taste great, too.

3. *Eat as many fresh fruits as you want.* Eat at least three fresh fruits daily. Minimize or avoid fruit juice because all or most of the fruit's fiber is lost in the juicing process. The full fiber available in whole fruits has valuable benefits and suppresses appetite. If you enjoy juice, it is better to drink vegetable juices. Add green vegetables to carrot, beet, or fruit juices to make them less sweet and more nutrient-rich.

4. *Eat a huge portion of steamed green vegetables with dinner.* Try to eat at least 10 ounces of broccoli, kale, string beans, artichokes, brussels sprouts, spinach, Swiss chard, cabbage,

asparagus, collards, okra, or zucchini. These can be flavored with stewed tomatoes, garlic, onions, mushrooms, and spices.

5. *Do not overeat cooked, starchy foods.* If you have heart disease or are overweight, limit cooked starches to one serving or one cup daily (such as one corn on the cob, one baked potato, or one sweet potato). Since there is no limit on the amount of low-starch plant foods you can eat, you'll never have to go hungry. There is some flexibility with these higher-starch vegetables; if you are not overweight, you can eat more of them. But don't overdo it.

Avoid refined carbohydrates, such as sugar, white rice, white bread, and white flour pasta. Oatmeal and steel-cut oats are permissible for breakfast, but even whole grains such as 100% whole wheat products should be limited to one serving per day.

More healthful starches (*one or two daily*)	Less healthful starches (*none to one weekly*)
turnips, parsnips	white bread
butternut and acorn squash	pasta
corn and sweet potato	white rice
peas and carrots	quick-cook hot cereals
wild rice and brown rice	tortillas and chapatis
quinoa and millet	cold breakfast cereals
steel-cut oats and oatmeal	pancakes and waffles

Squash, corn, sweet potato, and carrots are preferable to white potato and whole grain breads because they are richer in phytochemicals and carotenoids. Add them to soups, and serve them mixed with greens and beans. Depending on body weight and activity level, you might be able to eat a little more of the high-starch foods than someone else, but if you are trying to lower cholesterol, you still need to eat more non-starchy greens than starchy ones.

6. *Eat beans/legumes every day.* You can eat as many beans as you desire. Beans have a high nutrient-per-calorie profile, are very high in fiber, and help prevent food cravings. Throw a cup of canned chickpeas or other beans on your lunch salad. Make vegetable soups with beans. Canned vegetable and bean soups from the health food store can be excellent (look for the no-added-salt varieties).

7. *Animal products and dairy products should be eliminated or extremely limited.* If you continue to eat animal products, limit the amount to less than 10 ounces per week of white meat turkey, white meat chicken, or low-mercury fish (such as tilapia, flounder, sole, or scrod) per week. Non-fat dairy or an egg white omelette also may be consumed once per week as a replacement for either the fish or fowl. Animal products are best used as condiments to add flavor to soups, vegetables, beans, or tofu, rather than as main dishes. Low-mercury fish is preferable to other animal foods because it is lower in calories and saturated fat, and some of the fat is healthful EPA and DHA, the long-chain omega-3 fats that have shown beneficial effects on brain function. Fish also has a higher nutrient-per-calorie ratio than other animal foods.

For optimal heart attack protection and maximal cholesterol lowering, it is best to avoid animal products entirely. Sometimes even a small portion of an animal product in the diet can inhibit achieving maximal results because animal protein and saturated fat promote higher cholesterol levels.

Consuming one or two small servings of low-saturated-fat animal products each week, while otherwise following the *Eat to Live* recommendations, does not prevent most individuals from achieving and maintaining LDL cholesterol levels below 100. If you use a small amount of cow's milk, use only the fat-free type, and be sure to count it when calculating your 10-ounces-per-week limit. This near vegetarian style of eating is more acceptable to many people, and it is still an effective approach to heart disease prevention. However, if you are a person with known heart disease or significant cholesterol elevation, or have a family history of heart disease and another risk factor (such as high blood pressure), I strongly recommend that you eliminate all animal products to maximize your potential for disease reversal. A vegan diet with supplemental DHA fat offers you the most protection.

8. *Eat one tablespoon of ground flaxseed every day.* This will provide those hard-to-find omega-3 fats that protect against cancer. Flaxseed also contains many other heart disease and cancer-fighting substances, such as lignans, flavonoids, sterols, and fibers. To get all of the benefits, eat only the ground seeds, not flaxseed oil. Flaxseed can be ground in a coffee grinder or VitaMix machine. If you purchase flaxseed already ground, store it in a closed container in the freezer to preserve freshness.

9. *Consume nuts, seeds, and avocados in limited amounts.* Raw nuts and seeds are nutrient-rich, high-fat foods. For most people who exercise regularly and are not overweight, two ounces of raw nuts or seeds per day is not too much. Walnuts in particular are rich in omega-3 fats and heart disease-fighting compounds.

At one time, nuts were thought to be an unhealthful food because of their high fat content. However, recent evidence suggests that frequent consumption of nuts is protective against heart disease. Five large studies (the Adventist Health Study, the Iowa Women

Health Study, the Nurses' Health Study, the Physicians' Health Study, and the CARE Study) examined the relationship between nut consumption and the risk of coronary heart disease, and all found an inverse association. People who consume nuts regularly experience only about half as many heart attacks as nonconsumers.[44] The consumption of nuts also has been shown to reduce sudden cardiac death, cancer, and all-cause mortality,[45] meaning they significantly extend human life span. Several clinical studies have observed beneficial effects of diets high in raw nuts to lower LDL cholesterol levels.[46] Based on the data from the Nurses' Health Study, it has been estimated that if the people eating "average diets" used the fat from one ounce of nuts to replace an equivalent caloric amount of carbohydrates, there would be a 30% reduction in coronary heart disease risk, and if they substituted the nut fat for saturated fat, there would be a 45% reduction in risk.

You can eat between one and two ounces of raw nuts and seeds each day, but only about one ounce per day if you are overweight. Keep in mind that nuts and seeds have about 175 calories per ounce; therefore, overeating them could sabotage your weight loss and prevent you from achieving optimal results. One ounce is about 10 walnut halves, 15 cashews, 20 almonds, 7 brazil nuts, 18 pecan halves, 10 macadamia nuts, 20 hazelnuts, or 40 pistachios. Do not roast or salt the nuts (although they may be lightly toasted) because if they are cooked too much, the many beneficial compounds in them are destroyed. Raw nuts and seeds are healthful foods and have anticancer properties. They are ideal foods for kids, athletes, and those who want to gain weight.

Avocados are another healthful, high-fat, high-nutrient food that can replace any low-nutrient fats (such as margarine, butter, oil, cheese, and meat) that you were eating previously. Limit avocado to one-half daily if overweight. Like nuts and seeds, avocados can be used to make great-tasting salad dressings that deliver a full complement of antioxidants and phytochemicals in a particularly delicious form.

10. *The goal is to have at least 90% of your dietary intake come from nutrient-dense foods.* Vegetables, beans, fruits, nuts, and seeds are nature's nutrient-rich natural foods. Your meals need to revolve around these foods, not grains, oils, or animal products. Limit (no more than once a week) or eliminate processed foods, refined breads, and pasta.

It will help if most of your starch consumption comes from starchy vegetables—such as butternut or acorn squash, corn, turnips, parsnips, carrots, peas, and sweet potatoes, rather than from flour products. Brown and wild rice are better choices than flours—even whole grain flours—because they are in their whole form. The finer grain is ground, and the more it dries out during baking, the more toxic compounds, such as acrylamides, are formed. Eat little or no bread, and when you do have bread, choose the more coarsely ground brands, such as Alvarado Street. If you eat bread, whole-wheat pita is a good choice because it is less bread and it can hold a healthful stuffing, such as vegetables and bean spreads.

Avoid unhealthful desserts completely, or limit them to once monthly. The best dessert is fruit, or frozen fruit, whipped with orange juice or a little soy milk. You can add a frozen banana or a date for more sweetness, if desired. It is like eating ice cream, except it is good for you. In my house, we frequently blend a bag of frozen strawberries with a peeled orange and a slice of dried pineapple to make a refreshing creamy strawberry sorbet for an evening dessert. A few of my Date Nut Pop'ems (available from www.DrFuhrman.com) also make a great dessert. They are made from ground nuts and seeds and sweetened with dates.

Your basic cholesterol-lowering menu

Use the meal outlines below to devise menu plans and decide what to eat. Planning ahead helps you stay on track. Keep things simple. You do not have to prepare fancy recipes all of the time. If you're going to be out of the house, just make a sandwich from some leftover vegetables (or a box of frozen broccoli, peas, or corn), lettuce, and tomato on whole-grain bread—or stuffed into a whole-wheat pita pocket—and a few pieces of fruit.

Breakfast: *fresh fruit and/or oatmeal with ground flaxseed*
Lunch: *salad, vegetable/bean soup, and fresh fruit*
Dinner: *salad, two cooked vegetables, raw nuts, and fruit dessert*

Prepare large quantities of food so that you don't have to start from scratch at every meal. Wash and dry plenty of green lettuce on the weekends or when you have the time. Then, it will be easy to grab some fresh fruit, a bag full of lettuce, a vinegar-based dressing, and a box of frozen peas or a can of beans to add to the salad when you are late and running out the door to work or school.

In our house, we make a giant pot of vegetable and bean soup at least once a week. We divide the finished soup into about 10 separate containers and store them in the refrigerator. My typical lunch consists of one container of soup, leftovers from dinner, and some fresh fruit.

The most healthful way to cook vegetables is in soup. Eating raw vegetables is super healthful, but you are not able to absorb all of the available food value. You absorb more phytochemicals when you cook the vegetables in a soup because the gentle, water-based heating softens the cell walls, making nutrients more bioavailable without damaging them. Put your favorite beans, lentils, split peas, and spices in the pot, add water and vegetables, and cook on a very low flame. I like to start with freshly made juice (carrot, tomato, celery, or beet) to which I add lots of vegetables and leafy greens. When the greens get tender, I blend them and stir them back into the soup to make it thick and creamy.

Avoiding salt

As mentioned previously, salt is linked to hypertension and increased cardiovascular disease. All salts—sea salt, Celtic salt, and other so-called "natural" salts—carry the same dangerous risks. Eliminating salt from your diet is a powerful step in the direction of heart health. Initially, however, it may reduce your enjoyment of eating. High salt intake "deadens" your taste buds, and unsalted food may taste bland. Fortunately, your ability to taste the subtle flavors in vegetables will increase over time, and after 6-12 weeks without salt, simple, natural foods will taste better than you ever would have imagined.

Restored health

Eating according to the *Eat to Live* guidelines is a potent means of restoring your health. In fact, with the help of your doctor, this nutritional program can help you to slowly reduce or eventually eliminate your dependency on drugs. It has helped others avoid open-heart surgery and other invasive procedures, and it can help you. In fact, it could save your life.

The transition to nutritional excellence may seem a little

Heart-protective diet in a nutshell

About 90% of your diet must come from high-nutrient foods. Below is a list of the most healthful food categories. You can eat unlimited quantities of foods in groups 1-4. Foods in groups 5-7 should be consumed in smaller quantities. Below the list is a description of foods that you should avoid entirely or severely limit.

1. *Green vegetables*—such as kale, Swiss chard, broccoli, lettuce, string beans, artichokes, asparagus, spinach, cabbage, and peas

2. *Beans/legumes*—such as chickpeas, red kidney beans, lentils, and adzuki beans

3. *Fresh fruits*—such as blueberries, strawberries, kiwis, apples, oranges, grapes, pears, pineapple, and bananas

4. *Non-starchy vegetables*—such as tomatoes, eggplant, peppers, mushrooms, and onions

5. *Starchy vegetables*—such as potatoes, sweet potatoes, yams, turnips, parsnips, butternut squash, carrots, and corn

6. *Avocados, nuts, and seeds*—such as filberts, almonds, walnuts, cashews, pecans, flaxseed, and sunflower and sesame seeds

7. *Whole grains*—such as brown rice, quinoa, amaranth, millet, oats, barley, and whole wheat

Eliminate or severely limit animal products.
If you eat animal products at all, eat only about 10 ounces of white meat turkey, white meat chicken, or low-mercury fish (such as tilapia, flounder, sole, or scrod) per week. Non-fat dairy or an egg white omelette also may be consumed once per week as a replacement for either the fish or fowl. Animal products are best used as condiments for flavoring other foods, not as main dishes.

Eliminate all processed grains and sweeteners.
Avoid white flour, white rice, processed breakfast cereals, and sugar or other sweeteners. If using pasta occasionally, use whole wheat, brown rice, bean, or lentil pasta, not white flour pasta.

daunting at first, since developing new habits and new taste preferences takes time. But as you begin to feel better and regain your youthful vigor, your desire and ability to do what is necessary to totally protect yourself from heart disease and stroke will grow by leaps and bounds.

Dear Dr. Fuhrman,

The results of the *Eat to Live* program are beyond my wildest dreams.

My family and I are recovering from various health problems that have plagued us for years.

After three months on your program, my weight has leveled off at 155, which is perfect for my height (5'10"). Previously, I couldn't get my weight below the 180s.

My cholesterol dropped from 275 to 147. Amazing!

I gave your book to several people at work. They read it and are enjoying substantial weight loss, too.

Thanks for everything.

Sincerely,

Alan Markus

Chapter

7

Menus and Recipes

The seven days of plant-based menu plans and recipes that follow are totally vegetarian or vegan. If you want to add small amounts of animal products as condiments for occasional variety, you can still utilize these same menus and recipes.

Many more recipes and meal plans are available in my other books—*Eat to Live* and *Disease-Proof Your Child*, in my *Healthy Times* newsletters, and in the Member Support Center at my website: www.DrFuhrman.com.

All of the individual foods and recipes can be interchanged and eaten in other combinations and at different meals. While each of the meals that follow includes numerous tasty and interesting recipes, in the real world we don't always have time to prepare such delicious variety. Rest assured, you always can substitute fresh fruit, frozen fruit, or frozen vegetables (such as corn and peas) for a more complex dish, with little or no preparation time.

To save time, you can make extra helpings of a dinner recipe and eat the leftovers at lunch the next day, along with a salad and some fruit. When we make soup at our house, we make a very large pot of it, so that we can use it for lunches for the next 4-5 days. With a little ingenuity, you can use the following plans to create enough great recipes for months. For example, smoothies can be enjoyed as breakfasts, lunches, and dinners, and even as desserts! The same is essentially true of all of the recipes.

Some of the recipes below utilize Dr. Fuhrman's VegiZest (a very low-sodium vegetable seasoning mix) and flavored vinegars (such as Spicy Pecan, D'Anjou Pear, and Black Fig) to add a gourmet flair to a salad or other dish. These items are available in better food stores, as well as on my website: www.drfuhrman.com.

A Week of Meal Plans

Some of the menu items listed below are so easy to prepare that no instructions are necessary. Recipes that are followed by page numbers are described in detail in the "Recipes" section that follows.

Day One

Breakfast:
Familia (unsweetened) cereal with unsweetened soy milk
Fresh or frozen berries (blueberries, strawberries, blackberries, or raspberries)

Lunch:
Spinach Salad with Mushrooms & Oranges *(p. 96)* with Orange-Cashew Dressing *(p. 97)*
Whole-wheat Pita Pocket with Lettuce, Tomato, and Eggplant Hummus Spread *(p. 105)*
1 or 2 pieces of fresh fruit

Dinner:
Indian Mango Salad *(p. 95)*
Steamed Swiss chard and zucchini, with onions, mushrooms, and stewed tomatoes
Spaghetti Squash Primavera *(p. 108)*
Pears L' Orange *(p. 113)*

Day Two

Breakfast:
Citrus Medley—orange, pineapple, and grapefruit
Raw Cinnamon-Apple Oatmeal *(p. 90)* with flaxseed
   and walnuts (optional)

Lunch:
Greek Chickpea Salad *(p. 95)*
Butternut Smoothie Soup *(p. 100)*
1 or 2 pieces of fresh fruit

Dinner:
Garden Salad *(p. 93)* with Spicy Russian Dressing *(p. 97)*
Green Beans Pecandine *(p. 104)*
Sweet Potato Fries *(p. 106)*
Bluevado Pie *(p. 111)*

Day Three

Breakfast:
Mixed Berry Freeze *(p. 92)* with ground flax

Lunch:
Very Veggie Salad *(p. 96)* with D' Anjou Pear vinegar and
   sliced pears
Split Pea and Carrot Soup *(p. 101)*
Fresh fruit

Dinner:
Spinach-Strawberry Salad *(p. 94)* with Cashew-Currant Dressing
   (p. 98)
Chinese Apricot Stir Fry *(p. 103)*
Brown Basmati Rice with VegiZest seasoning
Wild Apple Crunch *(p. 112)*

Day Four

Breakfast:
Fruits & Nuts Oatmeal *(p. 91)*
Orange Goji Berry Smoothie *(p. 91)* or Chocolate Smoothie *(p. 92)*

Lunch:
Creamed Black Fig Salad *(p. 94)*
Sweet Beet Soup *(p. 100)*
Fresh fruit

Dinner:
Garden Salad *(p. 93)* with orange slices and lemon and
    Tahini Dressing *(p. 98)*
Steamed string beans with onions and mushrooms
Swiss Chard & Beans Italiano *(p. 105)*
Mango Riesling Compote *(p. 113)*

Day Five

Breakfast:
Eat Your Greens & Fruit Smoothie *(p. 91)*

Lunch:
Big Chopped Salad *(p. 93)* with Savory Tomato-Almond
    Dressing *(p. 99)*
Creamy Vegetable Soup *(p. 101)*
Fresh fruit

Dinner:
Jicama Salad *(p. 97)* with avocado and D'Anjou Pear vinegar
Golden Vegetable Stew *(p. 107)* or Baked Tofu Pizza *(p. 103)*
Orange-Banana-Berry Smoothie *(p.111)*

Day Six

Breakfast:
1 slice sprouted multi-grain bread
1 Tbsp. raw almond or cashew butter with
    mashed banana as a spread
10 oz. vegetable juice (carrots, strawberry, and
    mixed greens)

Lunch:
Tossed Mixed Greens & Fruit *(p. 95)* with
    Creamy Blueberry Dressing *(p. 99)*
Quick Vegetable Bean Soup *(p. 102)*
Fresh fruit

Dinner:
Mixed Green Salad *(p. 96)* with Pistachio-Mustard
    Dressing *(p. 98)*
No Pasta Vegetable Lasagna *(p. 110)*
Chocolate Smoothie *(p. 92)*

Day Seven

Breakfast:
Special Oatmeal *(p. 90)*
6 oz. pomegranate juice

Lunch:
Everything Salad *(p. 94)* with Orange-Cashew Dressing *(p. 97)*
French Minted Pea Soup *(p. 99)*
Fresh fruit

Dinner:
Cauliflower-Spinach Mashed "Potatoes" *(p. 104)*
Leslie's Winter Portobello Mushroom Stew *(p. 106)*
Vibrant Veggies *(p. 109)*
Pomegranate Poached Pears *(p. 112)*

Breakfasts

Raw Cinnamon-Apple Oatmeal
1 cup rolled oats
1 apple peeled, cored, and diced
1/2 tsp. cinnamon
2 Tbsp. black raisins or currants
1/4 cup unsweetened soy milk
1 Tbsp. ground flaxseed
2 cups water

Soak oats, raisins, and ground flax overnight in the water and soy milk. Mix in the chopped apple and cinnamon in the morning.
Serves 2.

Special Oatmeal
1 cup rolled oats
8 whole pitted dates, chopped
1/2 cup dried unsulfured apricots, chopped
1/4 tsp. coriander
3 cups water (add more during baking if needed)
1 sliced banana
1 apple, cut in chunks
1 Tbsp. ground flaxseed
2 cups frozen (defrosted) blueberries

Preheat oven to 350 degrees. In a baking dish, combine all ingredients, except for the bananas, apple, flaxseed, and blueberries. Bake uncovered for 30 minutes. Add banana and more water if desired. Bake another 15 minutes. Stir in blueberries and apples. Sprinkle flaxseed on top and serve.
Serves 4.

Orange-Goji Berry Smoothie

1/2 cup soy milk
5 oz. spinach (1 bag baby spinach)
1/2 cup frozen blueberries
2 medium oranges or tangerines, peeled, seeds removed
1/4 cup goji berries, soaked in soy milk overnight
1 whole banana

Blend soy milk and spinach until liquefied. Add remaining ingredients and blend until smooth and creamy.
Serves 2.

Fruits & Nuts Oatmeal

1/3 cup rolled oats
1 2/3 cups water
1/4 tsp. cinnamon
1 apple, chopped or grated
2 Tbsp. currants
1 banana, sliced
1 cup frozen blueberries
2 Tbsp. chopped walnuts

In a saucepan, combine water with the cinnamon, oats, and currants. Simmer until oatmeal is creamy. Add blueberries and banana, stirring until hot. Mix in apples and nuts and serve.
Serves 2.

Eat Your Greens & Fruit Smoothie

1/4 cup soy milk
1/4 cup pomegranate juice
5 oz. fresh spinach
1 medium banana
1 cup frozen blueberries
1 Tbsp. ground flaxseed

Liquefy first 3 ingredients in blender. Add remaining ingredients and blend until smooth and creamy. Adding or substituting other fresh or frozen fruits makes for nice variations.
Serves 2.

Mixed Berry Freeze

1/2 banana
10 oz. frozen berries
1/4 cup soy milk
2 Tbsp. ground flaxseed

Peel and freeze ripe bananas in a plastic bag or kitchenware. This is a good way to make sure no bananas go to waste—just freeze the ones that start to get too ripe. Place the soy milk in the food processor, with the S blade in place (or a blender). Turn the machine on and drop in small slices of frozen banana, one by one, and then add the berries. The same recipe can be made with other frozen fruit. Mix in the ground flaxseed and serve.

Serves 2.

Chocolate Smoothie

5 oz. organic baby spinach
1/2 cup soy milk
1/2 cup pomegranate juice
1 medium banana
1 Tbsp. natural unsweetened cocoa powder
2 cups frozen blueberries
1 Tbsp. flaxseed, ground

First, liquefy spinach in soy milk and pomegranate juice in blender. Add all remaining ingredients and blend until smooth.

Serves 2.

Salads

Garden Salad

1 small head romaine, Bibb, or red leaf lettuce
1 cup cherry tomatoes, halved
2 Kirby cucumbers, halved lengthwise and sliced
4 medium grated carrots
1 small avocado, peeled, halved, and sliced
1/2 cup raw pumpkin seeds
1/2 cup chopped green onions
2 whole red bell peppers, thinly sliced

Place greens and vegetables on a plate. Arrange avocado slices on top. Sprinkle with grated carrots and pumpkin seeds.

Serves 2.

Big Chopped Salad

1 medium head romaine lettuce, washed, dried, and
  chopped into bite-sized pieces
1 red bell pepper, chopped
1 cup no-salt canned garbanzo beans
3 stalks celery, chopped
1/2 cup purple onion, thinly sliced
1/2 cucumber, cubed
1 tomato, coarsely chopped
1 avocado, cubed

Toss all ingredients.

Serves 2.

Creamed Black Fig Salad
5 oz. package of baby spinach
5 oz. package of baby romaine
1 avocado
1/2 cup unsweetened soy milk
6 dried black Mission figs
4 Tbsp. Black Fig vinegar
4 ice cubes

Blend the avocado and soy milk together, and then add the rest of the ingredients to the blender or VitaMix machine until creamy smooth. If using a regular blender, use a carrot stick (if necessary) as a tool to ensure that the ingredients get completely blended.
Serves 2.

Spinach-Strawberry Salad
5 oz. baby spinach
3 oz. romaine
12 oz. frozen strawberries

Pile the lettuce and spinach leaves on a plate and lay the defrosted strawberries on top. Pour the juice from the thawed strawberries over the greens.
Serves 2.

Everything Salad
1 small head romaine
5 oz. baby salad mix
1 cup watercress
1/4 cup dried unsweetened cherries
1/4 cup dried unsulfured apricots, coarsely chopped
1/2 cup walnuts, coarsely chopped
1 cup fresh tangerine sections
1 cup sliced fresh strawberries
1/2 cup sesame seeds, lightly toasted

Arrange ingredients on a platter.
Serves 4.

Greek Chickpea Salad

16 oz. can of unsalted garbanzo beans
1 boiled potato, peeled and chopped in chunks
3 plum tomatoes, chopped
1/2 onion, chopped
1 green apple, peeled, cored, and chopped
3 Tbsp. Spicy Pecan vinegar
1/2 tsp. chopped cilantro
12 pecan halves, chopped
1 cucumber, chopped

Mix all ingredients together.
Serves 2.

Indian Mango Salad

1 red pepper, chopped
1 red onion, chopped
1/2 Tbsp. VegiZest (or other low-salt vegetable seasoning)
2 ripe mangos, peeled and sliced
2 firm tomatoes, chopped
Pinch chili powder
2 stalks celery, chopped

Mix all ingredients in a covered bowl and refrigerate.
Serves 2.

Tossed Mixed Greens & Fruit

1 large head romaine lettuce
2 kiwis, peeled and cut in chunks
1 pint fresh strawberries, cut in half
1 apple, cut into chunks
1 pear, cut into chunks
1/2 cup currants or raisins
3 Tbsp. chopped pecans

Toss all ingredients in a bowl. Sprinkle with chopped pecans.
Serves 4.

Very Veggie Salad

12 oz. baby romaine lettuce
1 cup cherry tomatoes, halved
2 cups lentils (or 15-oz. can), cooked and drained
2 whole avocados, cubed
4 medium grated carrots
1/2 cup raw sunflower seeds
1/2 cup chopped green onions
2 whole red bell peppers, thinly sliced
Leftover steamed vegetables (optional)

Arrange greens, vegetables, and lentils on dinner plates. Add grated carrots last. Sprinkle with sunflower seeds.

Serves 4.

Spinach Salad with Mushrooms & Oranges

5 oz. baby spinach (1 bag), washed
1/2 small red onion, very thinly sliced
4 oz. sliced white mushrooms
1 small can drained Mandarin oranges
1/4 cup lightly toasted sesame seeds

Arrange spinach and onions on a plate. Put mushrooms and oranges on top. Sprinkle with sesame seeds.

Serves 2.

Mixed Green Salad

12 oz. mixed baby greens
1 cup cherry tomatoes, halved
2 Kirby cucumbers, sliced into circles
4 medium grated carrots
1/2 cup raw sunflower seeds
2 whole red bell peppers, thinly sliced
Leftover steamed green vegetables (optional)

Arrange greens and vegetables on a plate. Sprinkle grated carrots and sunflower seeds on top.

Serves 2.

Jicama Salad

1 medium head romaine, Bibb, or red leaf lettuce
1 large jicama, peeled and cut into thin slices
2 Kirby cucumbers, sliced into circles
2 whole red bell peppers, thinly sliced
1/2 cup raw sunflower seeds

Arrange the lettuce, jicama, cucumbers, and peppers on a plate. Sprinkle sunflower seeds on top.

Serves 2.

Dressings

Spicy Russian Dressing

1/4 cup soy milk
4 oz. tomato paste
1 Tbsp. Black Fig vinegar
1/4 tsp. chili powder
12 blanched almonds
1/2 avocado

Make salad dressing by blending avocado, almonds, vinegar, soy milk, tomato paste, and chili powder.

Serves 4.

Orange-Cashew Dressing

2 medium oranges, peeled and seeded
2 Tbsp. Blood Orange vinegar (or rice vinegar and a dash of
    orange extract)
2 oz. raw cashews or 2 Tbsp. raw cashew butter
Squeeze of lemon (optional)

Blend dressing until smooth and creamy. Add orange juice to thin if needed.

Serves 4.

Pistachio-Mustard Dressing

1/3 cup raw shelled pistachio nuts
1 Tbsp. dijon mustard
2 Tbsp. VegiZest (or other low-salt vegetable seasoning)
1/4 tsp. garlic powder
1/2 cup unsweetened soy milk

Blend all ingredients until smooth in a (high-powered) blender.
Serves 4.

Cashew-Currant Dressing

2 oz. raw cashews or 2 Tbsp. raw cashew butter
1/4 cup unsweetened soy milk
1/4 cup unsweetened applesauce
Handful of dried currants or raisins

Blend the cashews with soy milk and applesauce to make the
dressing, or use raw cashew butter and mix until smooth. Add the
currants to the dressing and drizzle over the salad.
Serves 4.

Tahini Dressing

2 cloves garlic, peeled and chopped
1/2 cup tahini or pureed sesame seeds
2 Tbsp. VegiZest
1 cup water
1/2 cup fresh lemon juice
2 tsp. Bragg Liquid Aminos (optional)

Place all ingredients in blender. Blend until smooth. Sauce should
be the consistency of heavy cream. If too thick, add more water
and lemon juice.
Serves 4.

Creamy Blueberry Dressing

2 cups frozen blueberries
1 Tbsp. Spicy Pecan vinegar
2 Tbsp. balsamic vinegar
4 Tbsp. raw cashew butter
1/2 cup pomegranate juice

Blend all ingredients until smooth and creamy.

Serves 4.

Savory Tomato-Almond Dressing

1 cup no-salt tomato sauce
2 Tbsp. almond butter
1 Tbsp. Black Fig vinegar or balsamic vinegar

Place in a bowl and blend with a whisk. Add any additional seasonings such as garlic or onion powder if you like.

Serves 4.

Soups

French Minted Pea Soup

10 oz. frozen green peas
1 bunch fresh mint (save some leaves for garnish)
2 cloves garlic
3 Tbsp. VegiZest (or other low-salt vegetable seasoning)
3 pitted dates
Dash of Spike (or other no-salt seasoning)
3 cups water
1/2 cup raw cashews
4 tsp. lemon juice

Simmer all ingredients, except for cashews and lemon juice, for about 7 minutes. Blend soup until creamy. Serve garnished with fresh mint leaves.

Serves 4.

Sweet Beet Soup

4 cups water
1 can (2 cups) vegetable broth (low-sodium)
4 cups carrot juice
1 cup celery juice
3 beets, with beet greens (or spinach or chard)
2 medium onions
3-4 medium sweet potatoes or yams, peeled and diced
2 Tbsp. VegiZest (or other low-salt vegetable seasoning)

Put water, broth, VegiZest, carrot, and celery juice into a pot and simmer. Grate beets and onions with a food processor and add to the pot. Then add the bite-sized pieces of sweet potato and the sliced greens. Cook on low heat for one hour. Blend half the soup, leaving some chunky parts, so it becomes thicker and still has chunks of potato.

Serves 4.

Butternut Smoothie Soup

2 cups water
1 can vegetable broth, low-sodium
2 cups soy milk, original flavor
2 onions, cut in half
6 carrots, sliced in large slices
5 celery sticks, sliced in 1/2" slices
2 zucchini, medium sized
2 whole butternut squash, peeled and cubed
1/2-1 lb. fresh mushrooms, cut into bite-sized pieces
3 Tbsp. VegiZest (or other low-salt vegetable seasoning)
1 tsp. Spike or Mrs. Dash (or other salt-free seasoning)
1 tsp. ground clover
1 Tbsp. nutmeg

Put everything into soup pot except mushrooms. Boil and then simmer for 1/2 hour. Blend all ingredients. (Be careful not to over-fill the blender.) Add mushrooms. Cook another 1/2 hour.

Serves 4.

Creamy Vegetable Soup

4 oz. frozen chopped onions
8 oz. frozen broccoli florets
16 oz. frozen chopped collard greens
1 cup frozen edamame beans
3 Tbsp. VegiZest (or other low-salt vegetable seasoning)
2 cups carrot juice
3 cups no-salt vegetable juice
4 cloves of garlic, pressed or minced
1/2 tsp. ground ginger
1 can no-salt white beans (navy or cannelloni)
1 Tbsp. fresh lime juice
1/2 cup raw cashews

Simmer all ingredients except for collard greens, white beans, lime juice, and cashews about 45 minutes or until tender. In blender, puree cooked ingredients and cashews with just enough soup liquid to liquefy. Simmer greens in remaining broth for 10 minutes. Add pureed mixture and whole beans to greens and broth. Mix thoroughly and serve.
Serves 6.

Split Pea and Carrot Soup

6 cups water
1 package of split peas
2 lbs. carrots, peeled and sliced
2 bunches of Swiss chard or kale (or any other leafy green or broccoli)
4 medium zucchini
1 bunch celery, peeled and sliced
4 Tbsp. VegiZest (or other low-salt vegetable seasoning)
1 can unsalted vegetable broth (or 2 cups carrot juice)

Add all of the ingredients to a soup pot. Boil and simmer for 1/2 hour. Blend only the Swiss chard and zucchini with some of the soup liquid and place back in the pot. Simmer for another 1/2 hour.
Serves 4.

Quick Vegetable Bean Soup

1 lb. frozen Oriental vegetables
1 lb. frozen broccoli
1 lb. frozen mixed vegetables
1 cup frozen onions
1 lb. frozen collard greens
1 cup water
4 cups carrot juice
4 Tbsp. VegiZest (or other low-salt vegetable seasoning)
2 cans lentils (low-salt or no-salt)
1 can adzuki beans (low-salt or no-salt)
1 can red beans (low-salt or no-salt)
1 cup sun-dried tomato halves
1 lb. fresh organic spinach (baby spinach or coarsely
   chopped spinach leaves)
1Tbsp. garlic powder
1/2 tsp. ground coriander seed
1/2 tsp. garam masala (from health food store or mix
   yourself, see below)
1/2 tsp. curry powder (optional)
1/2 cup nutritional yeast (optional)

Combine all ingredients except for the fresh spinach and yeast. Simmer for 30 minutes. Turn off heat and add spinach and yeast and serve.

Serves 10.

Garam masala is a great spice that is made by mixing:

5 tsp. ground coriander seeds
1 Tbsp. ground cumin seeds
1 tsp. ground cloves
1 tsp. ground cinnamon
1 tsp. ground cardamom

Main Dishes

Chinese Apricot Stir Fry

2 blocks of extra firm tofu, cubed into bite-sized pieces
2-3 packages of frozen mixed vegetables
4 tsp. apricot preserves (100% fruit, no sugar added)
1 tsp. garlic powder
4 Tbsp. cooking wine
4 Tbsp. water
1 tsp. Bragg Liquid Aminos
1/2 tsp. Chinese seasoning, salt-free

Place 2 tablespoons of water and tofu in a pan and simmer on a low heat. Turn the tofu frequently to prevent sticking. In a cup, mix the apricot preserves, cooking wine, 2 tablespoons water, and the Bragg Liquid Aminos. Sprinkle half of this mixture over the tofu and continue to simmer. Defrost the frozen vegetables in a microwave or steam on stovetop. Once defrosted, add vegetables to the tofu. Sprinkle the remaining sauce over tofu-vegetable mix and add the Chinese seasoning. Continue to simmer until the liquid is largely cooked off.

Serves 4.

Baked Tofu Pizza

1 package extra firm tofu
1 cup unsalted tomato sauce
2 Tbsp. tomato paste
1 tsp. garlic powder
1 tsp. onion powder

Cut tofu into very thin sheets and place on a wire rack.

Mix the spices with the tomato paste and tomato sauce and spread over the tofu. Cook in oven at 325 degrees for 30 minutes or until tofu is yellowed on the outside.

Serves 4.

Cauliflower-Spinach Mashed "Potatoes"
6 cups cauliflower florets (fresh or frozen)
6 cloves sliced garlic
1/2 cup raw cashew butter
2 Tbsp. VegiZest (or other low-salt vegetable seasoning)
1/4 tsp. nutmeg
10 oz. (2 bags) fresh organic baby spinach

Steam cauliflower and garlic about 8-10 minutes or until tender. Drain and press out as much water as possible in strainer. Remove cauliflower and just wilt spinach in steamer and set aside. Process cauliflower, garlic, and cashew butter in a food processor with "S" blade. Mix well; the whole point of this process is to make the cauliflower creamy and smooth like mashed potatoes. Check the consistency. If it is too thick, add a tiny bit of soy milk, mix, and check again. Too much liquid and you will end up with soup (hence the draining).

Add seasoning and adjust to suit your taste. Mix pureed cauliflower with wilted spinach. Serve hot or warm. You may need to heat it quickly in the microwave before serving. Top with Leslie's Winter Portobello Mushroom Stew.
Serves 6.

Green Beans Pecandine
1 lb. green beans, washed, with tips removed
4 Tbsp. Spicy Pecan vinegar
2 oz. slivered almonds.

Lay almonds on silver foil and toast for two minutes in heated oven or on the lightest setting in a toaster oven. Mix the toasted almonds with the vinegar. Steam string beans and remove from pot and drain. Toss with the Spicy Pecan vinegar and almond slivers.
Serves 4.

Whole Wheat Pita Pocket with Lettuce, Tomato, and Eggplant Hummus Spread

Pita Pockets

2 whole wheat pita pockets

1 small head of lettuce

1 large or 2 small tomatoes, thinly sliced

Lightly toast or warm pita pockets. Add thin layers of lettuce and tomatoes.

Eggplant Hummus

1 eggplant baked at 350 degrees for 45 minutes

1 cup cooked or canned garbanzo beans (chickpeas)

2 Tbsp. tahini

2 Tbsp. lemon juice

5 cloves garlic, finely chopped

1/2 cup bean liquid (from the garbanzo beans) or water

1 Tbsp. onion flakes

Blend all ingredients in a blender until creamy smooth. Spread into pita pockets. (Also makes a wonderful dip for vegetables.)

Serves 2-4.

Swiss Chard & Beans Italiano

1 lb. fresh Swiss chard

6 cloves garlic, minced

15-oz. can no-salt tomato sauce

3 plum tomatoes, chopped

15-oz. can unsalted red kidney beans

Put all of the ingredients in a pot and simmer over a low heat until the Swiss chard is soft, stirring occasionally.

Serves 4.

Sweet Potato Fries

4 sweet potatoes
1 Tbsp. garlic powder
1 Tbsp. onion powder

Preheat oven to 400 degrees. Peel sweet potato and cut into strips. Lay on a non-stick cookie sheet. Sprinkle garlic powder and onion powder on potatoes. Bake approximately one hour, turning potatoes every 15 minutes.

Serves 4.

Leslie's Winter Portobello Mushroom Stew

1 large onion, chopped into 1/2" pieces
2 tsp. chopped rosemary
2 Tbsp. VegiZest (or other low-salt vegetable seasoning)
2 pinches of red pepper flakes
1/2 lb. Portobello mushrooms, sliced 3/8" thick
   (remove gills if you want a paler sauce)
1 lb. large white mushrooms, thickly sliced
2 garlic cloves, minced
3 Tbsp. tomato paste
1 1/2 cups mushroom stock or water
1 tsp. sherry vinegar
2 Tbsp. chopped fresh parsley or tarragon

Water sauté the onion and rosemary and cook, stirring occasionally, until tender, about 8 minutes. Season with VegiZest and red pepper flakes. Add the mushrooms and sauté until tender and juicy, about 5 minutes. Add the garlic, tomato paste, stock, and vinegar. Simmer gently for 12-15 minutes. Add the parsley and season with pepper.

Serves 4.

Golden Vegetable Stew

1/2 head broccoli florets, bite-sized
3 medium red bell peppers, coarsely chopped
1 small eggplant, cubed
1/2 head cauliflower florets, bite-sized
1 cup carrots, cut 1/2" thick
1 whole beet, cubed
1 cup celery, coarsely chopped
5 cloves garlic, chopped
1 large onion or 3 leeks, chopped or sliced
2 bunches kale, washed, removed from stem, and chopped
1/2 cup dried lentils, rinsed
1/2 cup split peas, rinsed
24 oz. can low-sodium tomatoes (chopped or crushed)
8 Tbsp. VegiZest (or a low-salt vegetable seasoning)
4 cups carrot juice
2 medium zucchini, cubed
4 tsp. cinnamon (optional, as needed)
1/2 cup raw cashews

Place all vegetables except for zucchini and enough water to keep from scorching in a large soup kettle. Simmer covered for 90 minutes or until vegetables, lentils, and peas are tender. Add zucchini and carrot juice, bring to simmer, and turn off heat. Blend 1/4 of the cooked vegetable mixture with cashews until smooth. Add blended mixture back into stew. This creates a creamy, chunky stew.

Serves 6-8.

Spaghetti Squash Primavera

1 large spaghetti squash
1/2 lb. fresh mushrooms, sliced
1 bell pepper, chopped
1 red pepper, chopped
1 medium onion, chopped
4 large tomatoes, finely chopped
2 cloves garlic
1 tsp. dried basil
1/4 tsp. dried thyme
1/2 tsp. Spike or Mrs. Dash (salt-free seasoning)
1/2 tsp. dried oregano
1/3 cup water

Slice the squash in half lengthwise, and scoop out the seeds. Place in oven at 375 degrees for 45 minutes. Bake until you can pierce squash easily with a fork. While the squash is cooking, sauté in water the onions, red and green peppers, garlic, and herbs. When the peppers are almost soft, add the mushrooms. When the mushrooms are tender, add the tomatoes and simmer about 10 minutes or until most of the liquid has evaporated. Spoon out the squash and top with the sauté.

Serves 4.

Vibrant Veggies

2 1/2 cups carrot juice
3 Tbsp. VegiZest (or other low-salt vegetable seasoning)
1 bunch broccoli florets
1 small head cauliflower, cut into florets
2 stalks celery, chopped
4 small zucchini, thinly sliced, lengthwise
4 small yellow squash, thinly sliced, lengthwise
3 medium bell peppers (red, yellow, or orange)
1 medium beet, peeled and sliced in strips
4 cloves garlic, chopped
1 whole onion, halved and sliced 1/4" thick
2 tsp. beet powder (optional)
1 tsp. herb de Provence (dried herbs)
1/2 Tbsp. Spike or Mrs. Dash (salt-free seasoning)
2 1/2 tsp. arrowroot (or cornstarch)
1/4 cup chopped parsley.

Mix arrowroot into carrot juice. Water sauté broccoli, onions, and garlic for 5 minutes. Add remaining vegetables and carrot juice-arrowroot mixture. Simmer covered, stirring occasionally (the sauce will thicken) until all vegetables are tender, about 8-10 minutes. Garnish sprinkled with parsley.

Serves 12.

No Pasta Vegetable Lasagna

2 large eggplant, sliced lengthwise into 1/2" strips
3 small zucchini, sliced lengthwise as thin as possible
3 small yellow squash, sliced lengthwise as thin as possible
2 bunches broccoli florets and peeled stems, chopped
4 cups mixed mushrooms (shiitake, button, and oyster)
4 medium bell peppers (red, yellow, or orange), chopped
1 bunch basil
4 cloves garlic
1 small onion, quartered
1 package silken tofu, firm
1 1/4 lb. tofu, firm
1/4 cup soy parmesan (optional)
1 cup mozzarella cheese substitute (soy cheese), grated
5 oz. (1 bag) fresh baby spinach, chopped
3 Tbsp. VegiZest (or other low-salt vegetable seasoning)
2 Tbsp. dried Italian herbs
3 cups low-sodium pasta sauce

Preheat over to 350 degrees. Bake eggplant slices for 15-20 minutes until flexible, but not completely cooked.

Tofu ricotta

Squeeze excess water and crumble regular firm tofu. Blend silken tofu, onion, and garlic until pureed. Add basil and pulse to coarsely chop. Mix pureed tofu and crumbled tofu, add VegiZest, Italian herbs, grated mozzarella cheese substitute, and soy parmesan.

Chopped vegetables

Sauté mushrooms and peppers for 5 minutes over high heat without water until tender.

Assemble

Spread a thin layer of pasta sauce on bottom of a baking dish. Alternate layers of eggplant slices, tofu mixture, squash/zucchini slices, and pasta sauce. Repeat layers, ending with tofu mixture. Spread pasta sauce on the top and bake for 1 1/2 hours or until very hot and bubbly. Garnish with shredded fresh basil.

Serves 8.

Desserts

Orange-Banana-Berry Smoothie

2 peeled oranges
1 banana
10 oz. bag of frozen organic strawberries
2 tsp. ground flaxseed

Blend until smooth in VitaMix, Blendtec, food processor, or high quality blender.

Serves 4.

Bluevado Pie

Crust:
6 date-coconut rolls (ground dates rolled in shredded coconut)
2 cups Familia (vegan, sugar-free muesli)

Knead the date rolls with the muesli and then roll the mixture out to make a thin crust for the bottom of the pie pan.

Filling:
10 oz. package of frozen blueberries
10 pitted dates, chopped
1 Haas avocado
4 bananas

Blend all filling ingredients together until smooth. (If you have a VitaMix, use it; otherwise use a regular blender.) Pour the mixture into the pie crust. Freeze for 30 minutes, then serve.

Serves 4-6.

Wild Apple Crunch

6 apples
8 dates
1 cup currants (or raisins)
1 cup water
3/4 cup walnuts
1/2 tsp. cinnamon
1/4 tsp. nutmeg
Juice of 1 orange

Peel apples and slice. Chop dates. Chop walnuts into small pieces. Mix all ingredients except the orange. Put in a covered pan and bake at 375 degrees for about one hour, or until all ingredients are soft. Stir occasionally. Sprinkle the juice of the orange on top. You also can make this on top of the stove in a covered pot.

Serves 8.

Pomegranate Poached Pears

6 medium pears
1 cup pomegranate juice
1 cup apple juice
1 whole cinnamon stick
6 whole cloves
1/4 cup chopped walnuts

Peel pears, leaving stems intact. Slice a little off the bottom of each pear so that they stand up. In a large saucepan, place pears standing up snuggly together. Pour in pomegranate and apple juice, then add cinnamon and cloves. Gently simmer, covered, for about 20 minutes, until pears are just tender. Remove pears and refrigerate until ready to serve. Remove cinnamon stick and cloves. Reduce poaching liquid over high heat until it becomes syrup. Chill syrup and serve over poached pears. Sprinkle with chopped walnuts.

Serves 6.

Mango Riesling Compote

3 mangos, cut into small pieces
1 cup unsulfured dried apricots
1/2 cup raisins
1/4 cup Riesling vinegar
10 oz. bag frozen peaches
1/2 cup unsweetened soy milk

Mix all ingredients together and marinate overnight in the refrigerator in a closed container.

Serves 4.

Pears L' Orange

6 pears of your liking
1/4 cup orange juice concentrate
1/4 cup white grape juice concentrate
1/4 cup pineapple juice concentrate
1 1/2 cups water
1 1/2 cups fresh cranberries
1 cup currants
2 Tbsp. arrowroot

Peel and slice pears. Put juice concentrates and 1 cup of water in a pot. Bring to a boil. Add fresh cranberries and currants, and return to a boil for 3 minutes. Reduce heat. Mix 1/4 cup cold water with arrowroot until smooth. Add to cranberry-currant mixture and stir until sauce thickens. Lay pear slices in a baking pan and cover with the sauce. Bake covered at 350 degrees until tender, about 35 minutes.

Serves 4.

Chapter

8

Dietary Supplements that Lower Cholesterol

Most people can lower their cholesterol to the ideal range through dietary changes alone. But not everyone. When nutritional excellence is not enough, additional means must be sought to ensure maximal protection. Prescription drugs that lower cholesterol can be used as an adjunct to dietary intervention, but that is rarely the best solution. Taking drugs invariably means taking risks. The side effects of drugs can be debilitating and sometimes deadly. Fortunately, safe natural alternatives exist, and they can be used in combinations that are just as effective as drugs. Generally speaking, prescription drugs should be a last resort.

While most natural cholesterol-lowering substances are advertised as safe and effective, some are more effective than others, and not all are risk-free. I recommend that only the safest and most effective natural compounds should be used.

There are numerous possible reasons why any individual's cholesterol levels do not drop to the ideal range, even after adopting the protective *Eat to Live* dietary approach:

1. *Because the healthful diet was not started until the individual was an adult, the human body's tendency to maintain the status quo (homeostasis) allows cholesterol production to*

continue despite a dramatic improvement in the nutrient density of the diet and the elimination of animal products. This status quo (called "set-point") for cholesterol production will drop over time, but that may take years.

2. *Saturated fats stored in the body as body fat and utilized as fuel during periods of weight loss may continue to fuel cholesterol production in the liver. As these fat reserves are utilized and the excess weight is lost, cholesterol levels will eventually improve, but, again, it may take years.*

3. *At a late stage of life (adult), genetic influences on cholesterol production may be too strong for dietary intervention alone to overcome.*

Superior diet necessary in all cases

If you are one of the individuals for whom dietary intervention alone (no matter how ideal and aggressive) is not enough, what should you do? There are safe and effective supplements that you can take, but the most important thing to do is to follow my *Eat to Live* dietary program as strictly and conscientiously as possible. Don't make the mistake of thinking, "Diet doesn't work for me, so I'll just take cholesterol-lowering drugs and eat whatever I want."

The only way to maximally protect against heart attack and stroke is by eating the way I recommend in this book. You also may need to take supplements or even (rarely) prescription drugs, but no amount of supplements or prescription drugs can offer maximal protection unless you also adopt a high-nutrient-density diet. Maximal protection only can be achieved if optimal cholesterol levels exist *in conjunction* with a cardio-protective diet. Simply getting cholesterol levels in the ideal range with drugs or supplements is not the same thing because without the benefits of a high-nutrient diet, you still will be at significant risk.

Cholesterol-lowering supplements

Let's review some of the natural agents that are sold to lower cholesterol. Not all of these substances are as effective as their promoters claim, and some have potentially dangerous side effects. They are presented in the approximate order of effectiveness, the least effective appearing first. I also will describe two unique supplements that I have developed, both of which contain the safest and most effective natural ingredients to lower cholesterol and promote heart health.

Garlic—Garlic is said to lower cholesterol. Several studies show a small drop in cholesterol, and other studies show no effect at all. A review of the best garlic supplement trials showed that it only produced a slight amount of cholesterol lowering.

Gugulipid—Gugulipid is an extract of the mukul myrrh tree that is native to India and is used in the Ayurvedic system of healing. It is advertised as a cholesterol- and triglyceride-lowering substance with no side effects, but it is relatively weak at lowering cholesterol. It supposedly works by increasing the liver's metabolism of LDL cholesterol. A review of the available studies showed that even at a very high dose, gugulipid is somewhat effective for some people and not effective for others. Dr. Philippe Szapary, professor of medicine at the University of Pennsylvania, did the only U.S. study on gugulipid, and he was surprised to find that it actually raised cholesterol in the majority of the 103 patients who took it.[47] My experience with patients who had tried gugulipid to lower cholesterol also was disappointing; I never saw a strong benefit.

Niacin—Niacin is effective at lowering cholesterol and triglycerides. But neither niacin, niacinamide, nor "non-flushing" niacin are ideal choices for lowering cholesterol because the massive doses they require to be effective produce the same side effects and risks as many drugs (including liver damage). Just because a product can reasonably be called "natural" does not mean it is nontoxic, and those on niacin therapy to lower cholesterol should have their liver function tests monitored periodically by a physician.

Niacin should be considered only after the safer cholesterol-lowering supplements have been implemented, and further cholesterol lowering is indicated. The upper dosage used to lower cholesterol is one gram, three times a day. The side effects of this high dosage can include: flushing of the skin, stomach irritation, diarrhea, ulcers, liver damage, fatigue, hypotension, and ocular side effects. The form of niacin that is safest to use with the fewest side effects is inositol hexanicotinate, although it is not as effective as the other forms.

Pantethine—Pantethine is the stable form of pantetheine, the active form of pantothenic acid (vitamin B5). It is utilized to manufacture coenzyme A (CoA), which transports fatty acids into the mitochondria of cells. Pantethine in dosages of 600-1200 mg daily has been shown to lower cholesterol and triglyceride levels 10-15% without significant side effects. It is usually taken as a 300 mg tablet two or three times a day. Some people experience diarrhea with increasing dosages. Pantethine should not be used if you are taking tricyclic antidepressants, antipsychotics, or drugs for Parkinson's disease because a reduction in the effectiveness of these medications has been observed. Pantethine can be used in combination with other natural cholesterol-lowering modalities for additional benefit. Pantethine can add an extra degree of cholesterol lowering if some of the more effective natural cholesterol-lowering agents I recommend are not, by themselves, adequate to reach the desired cholesterol levels.

Chinese red yeast rice—Chinese red yeast rice is effective for cholesterol lowering and reportedly contains a "natural version" of a statin drug. Even though this ingredient is "natural," its chemical similarity to statin drugs makes the use of this substance somewhat risky. As I already have stated, natural does not mean harmless, and there have been cases where this treatment caused muscle damage in renal patients, similar to the effect of statin medications. There is not enough long-term safety data available from which to gauge all of the potential risks.

Researchers have determined that the key ingredient in red yeast rice, called monacolin, lessens the production of cholesterol by inhibiting the action of a key cholesterol-producing enzyme in the liver (HMG-CoA reductase). This is the same way most cholesterol-lowering drugs work. When nine different red yeast rice supplements were evaluated in a recent clinical trial, the researchers found varying levels of the active ingredient. Total monacolin content varied widely, as did the type of monacolin used in each preparation. If you decide to purchase this product, be aware that the effectiveness and potential toxicity could vary considerably from brand to brand.

Plant sterols and stanols—Plant sterols and stanols are natural components of healthful foods such as nuts, seeds, and beans. The presence of these beneficial fatty compounds is one reason why eating beans and nuts effectively lowers cholesterol. The benefits of cholesterol-lowering plant sterols and stanols is one reason why I recommend that you eliminate refined oils and animal products from your diet and replace that fat intake with raw nuts and seeds, such as flaxseed, walnuts, almonds, cashews, sunflower seeds, and sesame seeds. Sterols and stanols naturally occur in these superior foods. If your cholesterol is still high even after adopting a high-nutrient diet, supplementation with sterols and stanols is a reasonable next step.

The cholesterol-lowering effects of these supplements are not as powerful as cholesterol-lowering drugs, but unlike the drugs, they have no known risks. These supplements are a good option for those who cannot reach the recommended LDL cholesterol level of 100 or lower with dietary changes alone. I think highly enough about the benefits of plant sterols that I have included them in the cholesterol-lowering supplement that I designed, LDL Protect, along with other effective natural ingredients.

A word of caution: Plant sterols and stanols recently have been added to fattening, unhealthful, processed foods (such as margarines) that contain hydrogenated oils, salt, food additives, and other harmful ingredients. Although these products are marketed as cholesterol-lowering, they contain competing ingredients, some beneficial, some harmful. A negative side effect has been observed in at least one of them. Researchers from The Netherlands-based Unilever, makers of Take Control® spread, reported that they have observed a 10% decrease in carotenoids in the bloodstream when processed food products containing plant sterols and/or stanols are consumed regularly with meals.[48] This could indicate that these products might be inhibiting the absorption of carotenoids from fruits and vegeta-bles. This decreased absorption has not been shown to occur when taking sterols and stanols directly as a supplement.

Pomegranate juice—Pomegranate juice is a rich source of phyto-chemicals and antioxidants that have been shown to protect against heart disease and cancer. Pomegranate juice not only low-ers cholesterol, it also lowers blood pressure and increases the speed at which heart blockages (atherosclerosis) melt away. A glass of pomegranate juice contains more antioxidants than either red wine, green tea, blueberries, or cranberries.

In a 2004 study, heart patients with severe carotid artery block-ages drank one ounce of pomegranate juice each day. After one year, their blood pressure dropped by an average of over 20%, and they achieved a 30% reduction in atherosclerotic plaque.[49] The plaque was measured by intima media thickness (IMT) technology. Medical studies have shown that the thickness of the plaque in a specific place in the neck has an excellent correlation with coro-nary artery atherosclerotic burden. The control group did not receive the juice, and their arteries closed off even further. IMT thickness increased 9%.

In addition to being good for your heart and blood vessels, pomegranates have been shown to inhibit breast cancer, prostate cancer, colon cancer, and leukemia and to prevent vascular changes that promote tumor growth in lab animals.[50] Pomegranates' potent antioxidant compounds also have been shown to reduce platelet aggregation and naturally lower blood pressure, factors that prevent both heart attacks and strokes.[51] Pomegranate juice also has been found to contain phytochemical compounds that stimulate serotonin and estrogen receptors, reducing symptoms of depression and increasing bone mass in lab animals.[52]

Given the fact that pomegranate juice is so rich in heart-protective compounds (and the benefits are so well documented), I recommend it for all patients with heart disease, high cholesterol, or high blood pressure, and I have added it to my cholesterol-lowering supplement, LDL Protect.

Policosanol—Policosanol is an extract from the wax of the sugarcane plant. (It also can be derived from beeswax.) Over a dozen well-designed published studies document the ability of policosanol to lower LDL cholesterol 15-20% and illustrate its safety. The phytochemical compounds found in policosanol also have been shown to inhibit lipid peroxidation, which leads to atherosclerosis.

Policosanol is extremely beneficial for blood vessel and heart health. It promotes cardiovascular disease reversal as documented by myocardial perfusion scintigraphy and Dopplar ultrasound.[53] Policosanol has been shown to be superior to cholesterol-lowering drugs in improving a beneficial lipid ratio and increasing blood perfusion to the lower extremities in patients with peripheral vascular disease.[54] Another recent study comparing policosanol to one of the strongest cholesterol-lowering drugs (atorvastatin) showed that policosanol achieved similar results in improving the cholesterol ratio and was more effective in raising HDL cholesterol.[55] The side effects and patient dropouts were noted in the atorvastatin group, but no side effects or dropouts occurred in the policosanol group.

Policosanol is the sole ingredient in many natural cholesterol-lowering formulas available today. It is safe and effective, and I include it in my LDL Protect.

Dr. Fuhrman's Supplements

I wanted to provide clean, safe, effective cholesterol-lowering supplements for my family, patients, and friends. When I couldn't find suitable products, I decided to design my own. I have formulated two unique supplements—**LDL Protect** and **DHA Purity.** I recommend them for all patients who have LDL cholesterol levels above 100. They are a natural complement to my comprehensive *Eat to Live* nutritional program. LDL Protect combines three effective natural cholesterol-lowering substances to provide powerful LDL cholesterol lowering without side effects. DHA Purity is made from vegetable-derived DHA and provides heart and cholesterol-lowering benefits without the negative effects associated with mercury contamination and rancidity found in DHA derived from fish.

LDL Protect

I designed this product specifically to meet the challenges of patients who want additional help in lowering their LDL cholesterol, but who do not want the risks associated with the use of prescription medications. LDL Protect contains policosanol, pomegranate extract, and plant sterols. I chose these ingredients because they are safe and have proven cholesterol-lowering effects. Taking this supplement can be beneficial even if you don't need to lower your cholesterol because it also protects against other diseases associated with aging, such as dementia and strokes. There are no known contraindications to the use of LDL Protect, and no adverse reactions have been reported for any of the ingredients in the scientific literature.[56]

Although my dietary recommendations are optimally effective for lowering cholesterol and protecting your heart, there are individuals who do not achieve the most protective LDL cholesterol levels without supplementation. If you begin a program of dietary excellence in childhood, you almost certainly will be assured of a perfect LDL cholesterol level throughout life. But if you start the program as an adult, the LDL cholesterol level produced by your liver may not reset to an optimal level (below 100) immediately; for some people, it could take years. Combining the dramatic cholesterol-lowering effect of nutritional excellence with the additional lowering effect of LDL Protect can make all the difference.

If you are overweight when you begin the *Eat to Live* program, you may see only modest improvement in your cholesterol level for quite some time. This is likely because your liver is still processing and utilizing saturated fats being released from your body's fat stores. This can continue until you reach your ideal weight. If you still have an LDL cholesterol above 100 mg/dL after conscientiously following the dietary guidelines in this book, I suggest that you add LDL Protect to your daily program. Two capsules per day deliver the recommended dose for effective results. For increased benefits, up to four tablets can be used.

DHA Purity

DHA is a fatty acid from fish and fish oil that lowers cholesterol. The benefits are well documented. But DHA from fish is an unsatisfactory source because most fatty fish contain potentially harmful pollutants, such as dioxin and mercury. Many people have reported difficulty digesting fish oils, and fishy taste, foul odor, and burping due to indigestion discourages people from using them.

To avoid the problems associated with fish and fish oils, DHA Purity contains only the most highly purified and concentrated DHA oil derived from lab-grown micro-algae. It is kept refrigerated from the time it is manufactured until it is mailed to you in a dark blue glass bottle (with a measured dropper), so that it is extremely fresh when it arrives. The clean, fresh taste with a slight lemon flavor makes it palatable and digestible without any burping or indigestion.

DHA Purity is the only natural vegetarian source of DHA harvested from algae that is dispensed in a measured dropper (which makes it possible to administer the correct dose to toddlers, children, and adults alike). Using a dropper rather than a capsule also makes taking DHA Purity easier for children, the elderly, or others who cannot swallow capsules.

DHA is an important part of your heart-protective dietary program. DHA also increases the elasticity of the blood vessels and reduces total vascular resistance, resulting in a lower pulse pressure that has significant effects at lessening the occurrence of cardiovascular events, such as heart attacks and strokes.[57] It also has an anti-arrhythmic effect, reducing the overall rate of fatal heart attacks.[58] Recent studies have shown that algae-derived DHA increases HDL/LDL ratio, decreases the total cholesterol/HDL ratio, and lowers triglycerides.[59]

DHA in vegetarians

Many vegetarians consume enough flax, hemp, walnuts, and greens (sources of short-chain omega-3 fat) to internally "manufacture" sufficient quantities of DHA fat (a long-chain omega-3 fat). But many do not. The benefits of DHA are too substantial to be ignored. Even people with seemingly ideal diets—from vegans to omnivores—have been found to be too low in this extremely beneficial compound.[60]

A recent study published in the *Journal of Nutrition* showed that when vegetarian subjects were given algae-derived DHA, their levels of EPA increased over 100%. (The human body can convert EPA into DHA, and vice versa.) This study also confirmed the ability of DHA to lower the LDL/HDL cholesterol ratio.[61] A higher level of DHA is thought to be the reason why populations eating some fish are found to have better LDL/HDL cholesterol ratios compared with vegetarians.[62]

I regularly draw blood tests to evaluate fatty acid levels in my patients to learn if and how frequently DHA deficiency develops. I have observed elderly vegetarian men, who were eating excellent diets containing nuts and seeds, develop neurological deterioration and tremors in their eighties. I believe this is due to DHA deficiency because 1) these patients all had exceptionally low DHA levels, and 2) their symptoms improved when they were given DHA supplementation.

With the availability DHA Purity, vegetarians and vegans can get all of the benefits of DHA (lower cholesterol, reduced heart disease risk, and prevention of neurological deterioration as you age) without any of the risks or hassles of fish oils. Supplementing your diet with DHA just makes good sense. My liquid DHA Purity supplies 187.5 mg of DHA with each recommended dose of .5 ml per day.

Chapter

9

Frequently Asked Questions

Is a vegetarian diet more healthful than one that contains small amounts of animal products?

Researchers do not know for sure. The preponderance of evidence suggests that either vegetarian or near-vegetarian diets are best, especially for patients with heart disease. In the massive China-Oxford-Cornell Study, investigators found that heart disease and cancer rates decreased as animal-food consumption decreased, all the way down to a mere 1.7 small servings per week. Below this level, there is not enough data available.

Some smaller studies suggest that adding small amounts of fish to a vegetarian diet is beneficial (a result of the well-documented benefits of increased consumption of DHA-fat from fish). The same benefits—plus the maximized reversal of heart disease—can be achieved with a strict vegetarian diet that includes flaxseed, nuts containing omega-3 (such as walnuts), and a DHA supplement. Whether you are a strict vegetarian or not, your diet still must be plant-predominant if you want to protect yourself against both heart disease and cancer.

Without question, the consumption of more than a few small servings of animal foods per week (even those low in saturated fat) will begin to increase cholesterol significantly. Population studies confirm that even this seemingly low level of animal consumption increases the incidence of heart attacks in susceptible individuals.

Most of my heart patients choose to follow a strict vegetarian diet because they don't want to chance the risks associated with animal consumption. By adopting a vegetarian diet that includes a supplement of DHA fat, they eliminate their chest pains (angina), increase their ability to exercise, and most often see a permanent reversal of their heart problems.

It is important to note that vegetarian or vegan diets do not supply enough vitamin B12 for most people. As a result, supplementation is essential. In rare cases, a unique individual who has a genetic need for higher amounts of non-essential amino acids (such as carnitine and taurine) might feel healthier if they add very small amounts of animal products to the diet. But this increased need can be met—without the risks of animal product consumption—by taking a supplement that includes the needed nutrients.

It also is important to make sure vitamin D intake is adequate. Those not getting sufficient sunshine to meet their vitamin D needs should take a supplement. Vitamin D deficiency is epidemic in America, and it contributes not only to the development of osteoporosis but to increased cancer and heart disease as well.

The diet and supplementation plan recommended in this book is designed to assure nutritional completeness and to help you achieve your maximal health potential. It is rich in calcium and iron from green vegetables, contains adequate protein, and is extremely nutrient dense.

How relevant is HDL level as a predictor of heart disease?

In people who have abnormally high LDL cholesterol levels, higher HDL cholesterol levels indicate some degree of protection. But the goal is not to have a high level of HDL cholesterol. Populations with the highest HDL levels also have the highest rates of heart disease.

Although it contradicts a lot of what you commonly hear, the goal is to have healthfully low levels of LDL cholesterol. Once that has been achieved, low HDL cholesterol is no longer risky. The populations around the world who enjoy complete freedom from heart disease as a consequence of their natural, plant-based diets have what most Americans would call "low" HDL cholesterol levels. How can this be?

The answer is very simple. When you drop your LDL cholesterol level below 100 as a result of nutritional excellence, your HDL cholesterol may drop as well. This lower HDL cholesterol level accompanying a substantial lowering of your LDL cholesterol level is not a risk factor for heart disease. When your arteries are not clogged up with cholesterol, there is no need for high HDL cholesterol to remove stored lipids within the plaque, and your body keeps the levels low.

When your total cholesterol falls to the ranges seen in the heart attack-proof populations around the world, your HDL cholesterol level no longer matters.

Is homocysteine level a reliable indicator of heart disease?

Maybe and maybe not. It depends on how high your homocysteine level is and the cause of the elevation. Homocysteine is an independent risk factor for heart disease. That means even if your cholesterol levels are favorable, heart disease can be caused by an elevated homocysteine level.

A high homocysteine level also can be a contributory cause of high blood pressure and place you at higher risk of stroke. Homocysteine can be elevated when there is a deficiency of vitamin B12, vitamin B6, or folate. It is rare, but still possible, for a person with a perfect diet and ideal cholesterol levels to develop chronic disease from an elevated homocysteine level.

Theoretically, most people eating a plant-based diet rich in vitamins, especially folate, need only consume adequate supplemental B12 to ensure a normal homocysteine level. However, there are some uncommon cases of individuals who have normal B12 documented by a methylmalonic acid (MMA) test and normal folate levels on blood tests, but who also have a very high homocysteine level. These people need to take extra folate because they likely have a genetic defect inhibiting the conversion of folate to its more active form.

After reviewing scores of medical studies on the relationship between high homocysteine and the increased risk of Alzheimer's, stroke, heart attack, and dementia, one has to conclude that there is a clear-cut relationship between high homocysteine and serious disease. However, this is a complex subject where lots of confusion abounds, and the correct way to lower homocysteine (or whether we should attempt to lower it at all) is still being debated. Clearly, further research is needed.

One reason there is such contradictory information in the scientific literature is because the researchers appear to have a poor working knowledge of excellent nutrition. As a result, they are not targeting the therapy to match the underlying cause(s) of the homocysteine elevation. Instead, they (along with most physicians) are giving the same conventionally designed nutritional supplement to all patients, regardless of the different underlying causes of the problem. This "one-size-fits-all" approach is too simplistic. Different causes require different solutions.

For example, homocysteine can be elevated from:

- *a poor diet, low in folate-containing vegetables;*
- *a vitamin B12 deficiency;*
- *kidney disease;*
- *an uncommon defect in conversion of folate to the active form (even in a person eating a healthful diet).*

Treatment approaches to various levels of elevated homocysteine need to be matched with the underlying causes.

Levels above 20 micro mol/l are associated with a tenfold increased risk of heart attack compared to levels below 9 micro mol/l.[63] These high elevations of homocysteine should not be ignored. Doing so could result in tragedy. Levels above 15 are an indication that B12, MMA (methylmalonic acid), and folate levels need to be checked. Mild elevations of homocysteine in the range of 10-15 do not appear to place people at higher risk.[64]

In most cases, elevations in the 10-15 range are merely a marker for an overall low-nutrient diet, and the correct treatment is to improve the entire diet—not just to supplement to lower homocysteine. Folate supplementation alone in these cases cannot compare with the value of actually eating a diet rich in folate and gaining all of the other essential cardio-protective compounds that are found in natural plant foods. It is similar to the mistake of taking a cholesterol-lowering drug instead of eating healthfully. A pill cannot take the place of the full symphony of dietary elements that contribute to heart and vascular health.

When elevated homocysteine is due to vitamin B12 deficiency, it is wise to take more vitamin B12. Vitamin B12 levels are considered normal in the 200-400 range, but even if you are in this range, you still could have a functional deficiency. The best way to determine if you are consuming sufficient vitamin B_{12} is to get an MMA test. If the MMA is elevated, a vitamin B_{12} deficiency exists—even if the vitamin B_{12} level in the blood is in the normal range. When vitamin B_{12} deficiency exists, extra vitamin B_{12} is the correct treatment for the elevated homocysteine.

If the folate level is excellent (15-25) and the vitamin B_{12} level is normal (as documented with a normal MMA), but the homocysteine is still significantly elevated, the cause of the elevation is most likely a genetic defect in folate conversion. In such cases, folate (or folic acid) supplementation may not be totally effective. This is because the patient is merely ingesting more of the folate they can't convert effectively to begin with. They don't need more of this folate; they need the more biologically active form (called methyltetrahydrofolate or formyltetrahydrofolate). Please visit www.DrFuhrman.com for further information regarding suppliers.

Is the H = N/C diet the best diet for everyone?

I do not recommend the same diet for everyone, but the H = N/C (health = nutrients ÷ calories) concept never changes. Not only do different people have somewhat different needs, the same individual may require modifications to the diet during various stages and situations in their lives. Furthermore, there are some unique individuals, such as elderly people, for whom an excellent diet and a multivitamin is not sufficient to supply their needs. These patients may have a greater need for certain non-essential amino acids and other nutrients, such as high-dose vitamin B_{12} or high-dose vitamin D. Fortunately, these needs are easily determined by blood tests.

There are illnesses (such as active inflammatory bowel disease)

A revealing homocysteine case study

Monroe Barberry, a slim, healthy 72-year-old, came to see me not feeling very well, and on his initial evaluation his blood pressure was noted to be 210/110. Monroe had been following a healthful, natural food, vegan diet, without salt, for many years, and he also was taking B12 supplements. His blood test did not show a vitamin B12 or folate deficiency, but his homocysteine level was 28. Since his blood pressure was so elevated, I had to use three separate medications to lower it into the normal range. Over the next year, Monroe's homocysteine level dropped to 12 with the use of a supplement of methyltetrahydrofolate and formyltetrahydrofolate. With the improvement in his homocysteine, his blood pressure returned to normal, and he was able to reduce and eventually discontinue the blood pressure medications. In this case, the high homocysteine was most likely the major factor causing his severe elevation of blood pressure. The elevated homocysteine was not merely an innocent bystander—it was a cause of disease. Clearly, in this case, the extra folate helped.

Presently, there are more than 10 large trials underway that will add more data to the current body of literature about homocysteine. In the meantime, it should be recognized that a vegetable-based diet rich in fresh produce with fruit, beans, raw nuts, and seeds, naturally low in saturated fat and sodium, is our most powerful protection against disease. It lowers blood pressure as much as drugs and, in heart patients, is at least twice as effective at reducing death rates and heart attacks as drugs.[65] The day may come when a physician who does not offer such a diet to his heart patients will be at high risk for being sued for malpractice.

that necessitate changes to dietary recommendations. Dietary guidelines always must be adjusted to match the individual's illness and digestive capacity.

I adjust and customize eating plans and nutritional supplements for individuals with unique medical and metabolic needs, and also for professional athletes. If you suspect that you have special needs, or if you need a healthful way to gain or lose weight, you are welcome to contact me for more specific advice.

Must I avoid chocolate, ice cream, and other junk food forever?

You can eat anything you desire—*on occasion.* Just don't make a habit of it. The desire to eat the foods you ate prior to adopting a program of nutritional excellence can be strong. Everyone is tempted by these foods. The easiest way to resist them is to get them out of your house. Completely clean out the refrigerator, freezer, and cupboards. If you are going to eat unhealthful food at all, only do it outside of your home. It is important to stick with your plan strictly during the first few months so you lose your addiction to toxic foods. Over time, your taste buds will change, you will begin to prefer the taste of healthful foods, and you will be less and less tempted by foods that undermine your health. Let the knowledge that you are protecting your health and future well-being be your guide. If possible, spend more time with friends and family who will support you in your efforts.

Is exercise essential for success?

Optimal results only can be achieved by those who exercise regularly. Not only does exercise help you reach your ideal weight, it also protects your heart and helps prevent and reverse atherosclerosis. Naturally, the amount of exercise you do has to be commensurate with your changing capabilities over time. You never should push yourself into pain or discomfort.

If you are ill or have specific physical limitations, break up your exercise program into three brief sessions matched to your needs. Many of my patients with angina begin their program by walking a relatively short distance (about five minutes) three times a day, increasing the time and distance gradually as their chest discomfort resolves.

Even if you start out with a low exercise capacity, by conscientiously sticking to the program, you will be amazed at how quickly your capacity and enjoyment for exercise increases.

Exercise will make you healthier, and it should be a consistent feature in your life. Some people complain that they just can't find the time to exercise. But we all know that they easily could find the time to eat an ice cream sundae or watch a favorite television show. If you feel short of time, take frequent five-minute exercise breaks— walk stairs, jump in place, or slowly alternate standing and sitting 30 times. As time progresses and you get healthier, I encourage you to join a health club and to use a variety of equipment, walk on an incline treadmill, use the elliptical machine, and utilize as many body parts as possible in different ways for maximum results.

I don't feel well when I eat this way.

When you change your diet to one that is significantly lower in salt and higher in nutrients, two of the things that will happen are: 1) your blood pressure will drop significantly, and 2) you will begin a detoxification process that can be compared to withdrawal from addictive drugs. It is not unusual to feel worse, not better, for a week or two.

During this temporary adjustment period (that usually lasts less than a week and rarely more than two weeks), you might experience fatigue, headaches, intestinal gas, or other mild symptoms as your body "withdraws" from your prior toxic eating habits. For example, eliminating coffee (or other dangerous, stimulating foods that contain caffeine) almost always causes temporary fatigue and headaches.

If you are on medication for high blood pressure or diabetes, you may require a gradual reduction in medications to prevent the dangers of overmedication, which could include your blood pressure or blood sugar becoming too low. If you are on medication for these conditions, please have your blood pressure and glucose levels monitored closely in the beginning—especially in the first few weeks—and have your medications adjusted accordingly.

I eat out a lot and will feel deprived eating this way.

Choose restaurants that have healthful options, and seek out ones that will cater to your needs. Whenever possible, speak to the manager or chef in advance. Most places are happy to accommodate you, especially when you state, "I am on a special diet prescribed by my doctor." It helps if you request a meal that includes foods that already are on the menu. For example, steak houses commonly serve salads, baked potatoes, and small portions of vegetables. Asking for larger than usual portions of these foods is an easily met request (be sure to tell them you do not want butter or salt). If you are going to the restaurant from your home, you can bring a favorite dressing or sauce to make the meal even more special and enjoyable.

No one can deny that it takes time for new eating choices to become pleasurable. But thousands of people have reported to me that over time they have come to prefer the taste of natural, plant-based meals. You will learn to enjoy healthful foods the same way you learned to like unhealthful ones...*habit!* Keep in mind, it takes some time for your taste buds to recover from having eaten a diet laden with salt. Salt deadens your taste buds. But once you are off salt for a few months, your ability to taste will be heightened, and the delicate flavors of natural foods will be more apparent.

If you find yourself in a restaurant or other situation where ordering a healthful meal is impossible, or if it would be significantly awkward or impolite, order the best meal you can and consider it a "treat"—one of those rare times when you eat like the bad old days.

My family, my friends, and my doctor argue that this dietary approach is not right for me. What should I do?

This plan is not for everyone. Despite all of the documented risks, many people choose to smoke cigarettes, eat unhealthfully, and pursue other reckless habits. Dangerous habits can be powerfully addictive, and some people would rather risk their lives than make the often substantial effort needed to free themselves. Like any caring person, I have empathy for people in those situations.

People have the right to live their lives however they choose. What concerns me about current-day American society is that most people do not know when they are making bad choices. When families, friends, and even doctors tell us that living healthfully (in a manner that is supported by the overwhelming preponderance of scientific documentation) "isn't a good idea," what does that say about us as a nation?

Clearly, people (including far too many physicians) do not know that dietary and other important lifestyle choices play the predominant role in determining health and well-being. People generally are not aware that it is possible to get well, stay well, and enjoy life without serious illness or the real threat of an early death. Instead, thanks to a thundering chorus of misinformation from food and drug corporations, government agencies, and disease-focused nonprofit groups, we are told that dietary choices have little effect on health and disease. We also are told that disease occurs by chance or (as is now the rage) by genetic inheritance, and that our only hope for health is wave upon wave of new drugs. This ill-conceived, ineffective advice undermines every person looking for genuinely lifesaving solutions to serious health challenges. When family, friends, and physicians merely parrot socially, politically, and commercially acceptable misinformation, millions suffer and die needlessly. Don't be one of them.

Family and friends aside, I have seen individuals violently reject my diet and health recommendations all on their own. This is a physical manifestation of a subconscious process. Our brains are designed to dim awareness to information that causes us anxiety, information that would require us to take action and make changes in our lives. Almost any change can be anxiety-provoking. Some people may fear the loss of beloved foods, alienation from friends and family, or some other distressing consequence. In response to these subconscious objections, many people choose to ignore or degrade the importance of the message. This phenomenon seems to be even more prevalent in individuals who don't think they have imminent health issues.

There are countless other diet programs that promise weight loss and good health without having to change the way we eat. This promise alone is enough to keep most of us from doing the hard work necessary to change; it gives our subconscious minds a way out. The allure to the subconscious mind does not have to be logical, and when misinformation about nutrition is popular, culturally accepted, and (as is often the case) endorsed by a celebrity, it is easily accepted by the ill-informed as truthful and effective.

Unhealthful foods are slow-working poisons. Many ailments related to poor food choices take years to develop, and these ailments often don't display visible symptoms until they are well advanced. The only visible symptom for most people is their excess weight.

Studies have shown that most overweight people routinely underestimate the extent of their obesity. They don't see themselves as overweight. With this in mind, it is not too difficult to understand why so many can ignore the evidence. They simply don't see that it has anything to do with them.

People react similarly to their heart disease risk factors. They ignore the threat to their lives posed by high cholesterol and do not act to protect their lives. Too often, the first real symptom they cannot ignore is death or severe debilitation.

The good news is that you do have control over your health and your weight. You are not at the mercy of your genes or your subconscious mind. You are not condemned by fate to develop the diseases other Americans (including your doctor) do. Heart disease, strokes, cancer, dementia, diabetes, allergies, arthritis, and other common illnesses are not predominantly genetic; rather, they are the result of incorrect dietary choices.

Disease and a premature death are not inevitable. They are the direct consequence of eating the disease-causing diet so prevalent in America and other modern societies. We dig our graves with our knives and forks. On the other hand, we have an unprecedented opportunity in human history to use science to live longer and to achieve health unobtainable by prior generations. All it takes is a decision to adopt a healthful, high-nutrient dietary program and to stick with it until it becomes your delightfully pleasurable norm. You are given only one body in this lifetime—take proper care of it!

Chapter

10

A Strategy for Success

"I know that nutritional excellence will lower my cholesterol and protect me against heart attack and stroke, but something in me still doesn't want to eat this way, and I am not sure why."

Countless people who have adopted my advice for nutritional excellence have reversed heart disease, diabetes, and auto-immune diseases. They have eliminated chronic headaches and migraines. Some have been brought back from the brink of death. Each of these recoveries can be traced to a series of simple acts. Someone—someone like you—learned how to make a few new recipes. Someone decided to try oatmeal or fruit for breakfast. Someone made sure always to have a few meals and snacks pre-pared in advance. Someone smiled and politely said, "No, thank you," at dinner, at the office, at the cocktail party. Simple acts, but courageous acts, too. A great many people are hesitant to even con-sider making such changes.

Thousands of case histories and thousands of scientific studies demonstrate the incredible benefits of adopting a high-nutrient dietary program. But despite this mountain of scientific evidence, change can be difficult, and some people are so addicted to their present dangerous diet that they would rather risk painful prema-ture death than change their eating habits.

It is normal to fear a loss of pleasure if you avoid favorite foods and accustomed dietary habits. But if you think that you *can't* change your eating habits, or that you will lose too much pleasure from life if you do, I want to assure you that you *can* do it, and that the sooner you make the changes, the sooner your new eating habits will become "normal" and pleasurable.

Understanding addictions

Knowing what to eat and how to live is not enough. You need to put your knowledge into practice. Consider cigarette smokers and drug abusers. They know that their habits are harmful; they know they should stop. Yet for reasons that even they cannot fully explain, they simultaneously believe they are better off continuing with their addictive behaviors.

How different is this from the way most Americans approach their diets? People know that a pasta-pizza-bread-butter-chicken-burger-sugar diet is harmful; they know fruits and vegetables are the healthiest foods on the planet. Yet for reasons they may not understand, they still believe that eating healthfully will somehow be less pleasurable than chronic disease and premature death. Most Americans are addicted to disease-causing food.

Addictive habits can take control of your life. If you don't feed your addiction, you feel poorly, both emotionally and physically. It can become as dangerous (but all-too-common) as this:

You get up in the morning and take a drug to get going. You need a caffeine or sugar hit, or you can't concentrate. After a few antacids to counteract your sour stomach, a stool softener, and a little mouthwash to tame your bad breath, you are ready to face the day...until a few hours later when the withdrawal headache starts to kick in.

As you age, it gets worse. Your life revolves around doctor visits, medical tests, procedures, drugs, and more and more suffering and misery. When you try to get off the coffee and disease-promoting diet, you feel even worse. Eating habits can be just as addictive as drugs.

The more stimulating your habits, the harder they are to break. The habits that are the most stimulating often are the most toxic; you feel ill and even depressed when you don't imbibe. For example, cheese, salt, and chocolate candy are all highly addictive, and it takes a prolonged period of abstinence to beat these addictions. Sugar withdrawal has been demonstrated to be similar to opioid withdrawal. Repeated intake of sugar creates neurochemical signs of opioid withdrawal, including anxiety and tremors.[66] Complex emotional and psychological factors also can make it difficult for some people to overcome food addiction.

Improved dietary habits can cause temporary (although they rarely feel temporary) physical changes that may discourage you. Eliminating caffeine, added salt, and saturated fat from your diet (while at the same time dramatically increasing your intake of high-fiber, high-nutrient foods) can result in unpleasant symptoms, such as headaches, fatigue, and other withdrawal symptoms, as well as increased gas. These withdrawal symptoms rarely last longer than one week. Most people find they sleep better, move their bowels better, digest food better, and enjoy life much more once they rid themselves of their toxic food habits.

Breaking an addiction is tough, but it only takes a few seconds of decision-making to win the battle. Simply decide to say an emphatic "No" to the addiction, and "Yes" to your new healthful diet and lifestyle. Remember, the ability to make the right decision consistently requires planning. You need time to prepare your environment so that you have good-tasting, healthful foods around you at all times. This minimizes temptation.

A taste of success

Frankly, I would eat the way I do even if it resulted in a decrease in food-derived pleasures, but after years of eating a high-nutrient diet, I unquestionably prefer the taste of healthful meals. Because I am consistent with my good eating habits, health-destroying foods are no longer even attractive to me. The same transformation will happen to you. I have seen it happen for thousands of people.

Over time, your desire for unhealthful items diminishes, and your tastes and preferences change. Once your body acclimates to the new way of eating, the taste of the greasy, heavily salted and sweetened foods becomes repulsive, and eating unhealthful foods will cause unpleasant symptoms.

Your tastes and food preferences are not fixed. They can change, and as they change, you begin to enjoy healthful food and healthful recipes as much or more than you enjoyed your prior way of eating. Before long, you will get more pleasure from the other parts of your life, too. Your improved health will make it possible for you to be more productive at work and at play. You will look better, feel better, and be better able to enjoy sexual activity. Whatever you enjoy—sports, travel, entertainment, exercise, work, or family, your renewed health and vigor will enhance that enjoyment. Your memory and intelligence will stay strong as you age, and you will experience a more enjoyable life.

Putting knowledge into practice

Just as you cannot expect to develop a perfect tennis swing or learn how to play a musical instrument without both good instruction

Dear Dr. Fuhrman,

After three heart attacks within three months of each other, and despite five angioplasties in a three-year period, I still was very ill. I almost died soon after the last angioplasty and developed internal bleeding that was difficult to stop.

The ongoing torture of all my health problems had me thinking that I would be better off if I had died. I had unstable angina, with chest pain from my bad heart almost all the time. I weighed 225 pounds, and I could not walk one block. I was on about 10 medications, and I was a cardiac cripple at the age of 60.

Luckily, I discovered your book, *Eat to Live*. I read it cover to cover and very quickly lost 30 pounds. Within three months after my first visit to your office, my chest pain was gone, and I was walking again—two miles with no problems. After seven months of following your high-nutrient diet, my weight was down to 135 pounds. I had lost 90 pounds *without even trying to lose weight*. I had just wanted to become healthier and to start living again.

When I think back to how sick I was, it is frightening. I was suffering from daily migraines and had developed bleeding ulcers from all the medications I was taking. Now I walk three miles each day, go to yoga and exercise class, and enjoy life immensely.

I am now 63 years of age, and I would not be alive today if it were not for you.

Judy Conrad

and a tremendous amount of practice, you cannot hope to transform your health without the ongoing process of putting your new knowledge into practice. Improving the way you eat and learning how to handle social situations that encourage bad habits are both part of an ongoing process of healthful change. These changes take time, effort, and the ability to learn from mistakes, but as the saying goes, "practice makes perfect."

As I stated earlier, it is not enough simply to "know" what to do. You need to *do it*. You need to practice preparing recipes and planning healthful meals until you get proficient at it, and the meals become pleasurable.

Anyone who has become accomplished at demanding activities such as sports, martial arts, and music will tell you that it can be difficult to learn new things. It is not easy to develop new habits, and there is no shortcut to developing new skills and expertise. To eat healthfully takes practice and perseverance.

Fortunately, when you do something over and over, it creates a pathway in the brain that makes it easier and more comfortable to repeat it again later. That is one reason why it is so hard to change. It can be really tough for a person with ingrained bad habits to change. For example, I would rather teach someone who never played tennis before how to properly swing a tennis racket than to try to teach someone who has been playing for years and swings incorrectly. But while change is difficult, it is not impossible. Change becomes possible when you have a strong desire and motivation to change, a willingness to endure the temporary effects of withdrawal from your bad habits, and the determination to work on the changes until they are mastered.

The more healthful meals you eat, and the more days of healthful eating you can string together, the more your brain will naturally prefer to eat this way, and your taste for healthful foods will grow. It has been shown that a new food needs to be eaten about 10-15 times before it can become a preferred food. Of course, it is faster, easier, and more convenient to eat fast food and junk food and eat out in restaurants, but this is what caused your problems in the first place. There are no shortcuts. Unless you make a concerted effort to learn healthful food preparation and take the responsibility of preparing it, you won't get the disease protection that you are looking for.

It takes extra time and effort to plan a week of healthful, satisfying meals. You need to purchase food in advance and to set aside time to cook and prepare the foods you buy. But if you make a commitment to your new plan for healthful eating, you will dramatically increase the probability of success. Rest assured—the results of your efforts will be richly rewarding.

An extraordinary opportunity

Compared to just a few years ago, there is a tremendous amount of scientific information available, lighting the way to high-level health and longevity. You are not alone in your efforts to transform a lifetime of bad habits into a new life filled with joy and vitality. Take advantage of all the support that is available to you. In time, you will become such a wonderful example of excellent health that others will be inspired to follow your lead.

I invite you to take advantage of the many support services offered at DrFuhrman.com. My support (as well as the support of an interactive community of like-minded people) is extremely helpful and can help ensure your success. On the website, you can discover new menus and recipes, read topical newsletters, complete tutorials on a wide range of topics, listen to live teleconferences, and participate in discussion forums. The lively "Ask the Doctor" forum is a place to ask questions (which I answer personally), plus you can read the answers to all of the previously asked questions.

Another unique and valuable feature of DrFuhrman.com is the ability to track your health progress online (complete with charts and graphs) and to store your medical records. Your medical records and health progress—such as lower cholesterol, lower blood pressure, weight loss, and other achievements—will be available online to you 24 hours per day, 365 days per year.

To contact Joel Fuhrman, M.D., and DrFuhrman Online, Inc.:

Toll-free order line:	(800) 474-WELL (9355)
Website:	www.drfuhrman.com
Medical office:	(908) 237-0200
Address:	4 Walter Foran Blvd, Suite 408 Flemington, NJ 08822
E-mail:	info@drfuhrman.com

References

1. Esselstyn CB. "Resolving the coronary artery disease epidemic through plant-based nutrition." *Prev Cardiol* 2001;4:171-177.

2. Sinnett PF, Whyte HM. "Epidemiological studies in total highland population, Tukisenta, New Guinea. Cardiovascular disease and relevant clinical, electrocardiography, radiological and biochemical findings." *J Chron Diseases* 1973;26:265.

   Campbell TC, Parpia B, Chen J. "Diet, lifestyle and the etiology of coronary artery disease: The Cornell China Study." *Am J Card* 1998; 82(10B):18T-21T.

   Miller K. "Lipid values in Kalahari Bushman." *Arch Intern Med* 1968; 121:414.

3. Breslow JL. "Cardiovascular disease myths and facts." *Cleve Clin J Med* 1998;65(6):286-287.

4. Gordon T, Castelli WP, Hjortland MC, et al. "Predicting coronary heart disease in middle-aged and older persons. The Framington study." *JAMA* 1977 Aug 8;238(6):497-499.

5. O'Keefe JH, Cordain L. "Cardiovascular disease resulting from a diet and lifestyle at odds with our Paleolithic genome: how to become a 21st century hunter-gatherer." *Mayo Clin Proc* 2004;79:101-108.

6. O'Keefe JH, Cordain L, Harris WH, et al. "Optimal low-density lipoprotein is 50 to 70 mg/dL. Lower is better and physiologically normal." *J Am Coll Cardiol* 2004;43(11):2142-2146.

7. Smilde TJ, van Wissen S, Wollersheim H, et al. "Effect of aggressive versus conventional lipid lowering on atherosclerosis progression in familial hypercholesterolemia (ASAP): a prospective, randomized, double-blinded trial." *Lancet* 2001;357:577-581.

   Taylor AJ, Kent SM, Flaherty PJ, et al. "ARBITER: Arterial Biology for the Investigation of the Treatment Effects of Reducing Cholesterol: a randomized trial comparing the effects of atorvastatin and pravastatin on carotid intima medial thickness." *Circulation* 2002;106:2055-2060.

8. Nissen S, Tuzcu EM, Schenhagen P, et al. "Effect of intensive com-pared with moderate lipid-lowering therapy on progression of coro-nary atherosclerosis: a randomized controlled trial." *JAMA* 2004; 291:1071-1080.

9. Heart Protection Study Collaborative Group. "MRC/BHF Heart Protection Study of cholesterol lowering with simavastatin in 20,536 high-risk individuals: a randomized placebo-controlled trial." *Lancet* 2002;360:7-22.

Cannon CP, Braunwald E, McCabe CH, et al. "Comparison of intensive and moderate lipid lowering with statins after acute coronary syn-dromes." *N Eng J Med* 2004;350:1495-1502.

10. Sacks FM, Tonkin AM, Shepherd J, et al. "Effect of pravastatin on coronary disease events in subgroups defined by coronary risk fac-tors: The Prospective Pravastatin Pooling Project." *Circulation* 2000;102: 1893-1900.

11. Grundy SM, Cleeman JI, Merz CN, et al. "Implications of Recent Clinical Trials for the National Cholesterol Education Program Adult Treatment Panel III Guidelines." *Circulation* 2004;110(2):227-239.

12. Watson KE, Fonarow GC. "Lessons learned from recent lipid-lowering trials: why physicians should change clinical practice." *Clin Corner-stone* 2003; Suppl 1:S11-17.

13. Forrester JS, Shah PK. "Lipid lowering versus revascularization—an idea whose time (for testing) has come." *Circulation* 1997;96:1360-1362.

14. Naghavi M, Libby P, Falk E, et al. "From vulnerable plaque to vulnera-ble patient: a call for new definitions and risk assessment strategies: Part II." *Circulation* 2003;108(15):1772-1778.

Naghavi M, Libby P, Falk E, et al. "From vulnerable plaque to vulnera-ble patient: a call for new definitions and risk assessment strategies: Part I." *Circulation* 2003; 108(14):1664-1672.

Wexberg P, Gyongyosi M, Sperker W, et al. "Pre-existing arterial remod-eling is associated with in-hospital and late adverse cardiac events after coronary interventions in patients with stable angina pectoris." *J Am Coll Cardiol* 2000 Nov 15;36(6):1860-1869.

15. Ornish D, Scherwitz IW, Billings JH, et al. "Intensive lifestyle changes for reversal of coronary heart disease." *JAMA* 1998;280:2001-2007.

16. Ambrose JA, Fuster V. "Can we predict future coronary events in patients with stable coronary artery disease?" *JAMA* 1997;277:343-344.

Forrester JS, Shah PK. "Lipid lowering versus revascularization—an idea whose time (for testing) has come." *Circulation* 1997;96:1360-1362.

17. Danenberg HD, Welt FG, Walker, M, et al. "Systemic inflammation induced by lipopolysaccharide increases neointimal formation after balloon and stent injury in rabbits." *Circulation* 2002:105(24):2917-2922.

    Hoshida S, Nishino M, Takeda T, et al. "A persistent increase in C-reactive protein is a risk factor for restenosis in patients with stable angina who are not receiving statins." *Atherosclerosis* 2004;173(2): 285-290.

18. Peters S. "Can angiotensin receptor antagonists prevent restenosis after stent placement?" *Am J Cardiovasc Drugs* 2002;2(3):143-148.

19. Jukema JW, Bruschke AV, van Boven AJ, et al. "Effects of lipid lowering by pravastatin on progression and regression of coronary artery disease in symptomatic men with normal to moderately elevated serum cholesterol levels. The Regression Growth Evaluation Statin Study (REGRESS)." *Circulation* 1995;91(10):2528-2540.

20. SJ Sharp, SJ Pocock. "Time trends in serum cholesterol before cancer death." *Epidemiology* 8: (MAR 1997):132-136.

    M Zureik, D Courbon, P Ducimetiere. "Decline in serum total cholesterol and the risk of death from cancer." *Epidemiology* 8:2(MAR 1997): 137-143.

21. Shirani J, Yousefi J, Roberts WC. "Major cardiac findings at necropsy in 366 American octogenarians." *Am J Cardiol* 1995;75(2):151-156.

22. Joseph A, Ackerman D, Talley JD, et al. "Manifestations of coronary atherosclerosis in young trauma victims—an autopsy study." *J Am Coll Cardiol* 1993;22(2):459-467.

23. Campbell TC, Junshi C. "Diet and chronic degenerative diseases: perspective from China." *Am J Clin Nutr* 1994;59(5 Suppl):1153S-1161S.

24. Ornish D, Brown SE, Scherwitz LW, et al. "Can lifestyle changes reverse coronary heart disease?" *Lancet* 1990;336:129-133.

25. Esselstyn CB Jr, Ellis SG, Medendorp SV, Crowe TD. "A strategy to arrest and reverse coronary artery disease: a 5-year longitudinal study of a single physician's practice." *J Fam Prac* 1995;41:560-568.

26. Ramsey LE, Yen WW, Jackson PR. "Dietary reduction of serum cholesterol concentration: time to think again." *BMJ* 1991;303(6808):953-957.

27. Lichtenstein AH, Van Horn L. "Very low fat diets." *Circulation* 1998; 98(9):935-939.

28. Menotti A, Kromhout D, Blackburn H, et al. "Food intake patterns and 25-year mortality from coronary heart disease: cross-cultural correlations in the Seven Countries Study. The Seven Countries Study Research Group." *Eur J Epidemiol* 1999 Jul;15(6):507-515.

29. Kromhout D, Menotti A, Bloemberg B, et al. "Dietary saturated and

trans-fatty acids and cholesterol and 25-year mortality from coronary heart disease; the Seven Countries Study." *Prev Med* 1995;24(3):308-315.

Oomen CM, Ocke MC, Feskens EJ, et al. "Association between trans-fatty acid intake and 10-year risk of coronary heart disease in the Zutphen Elderly study: a prospective population-based study." *Lancet* 2001;357(9258):746-751.

Lemaitre RN, King IB, Raghunathan TE, et al. "Cell membrane trans-fatty acids and the risk of primary cardiac arrest." *Circulation* 2002;105(6):697-701.

Kromhout D. "Diet and cardiovascular diseases." *J Nutr Health Aging* 2001;5(3):144-149.

Hu FB, Manson JE, Willett WC. "Types of dietary fat and risk of coronary heart disease: a critical review." *J Am Coll Nutr* 2001;20(1):5-19.

Lichtenstein AH, Van Horn L. "Very low fat diets." *Circulation* 1998; 98 (9):935-939.

30. Tang JL, Armitage JM, Lancaster T, et al. "Systematic review of dietary intervention trials to lower blood total cholesterol in free-living subjects." *BMJ* 1998 Apr 18;316(7139):1213-1220.

31. *Composition of Foods—Raw-Processed-Prepared.* Agriculture Handbook 8. Series and Supplements. United States Department of Agriculture, Human Nutrition Information Service; Minnesota Nutrition Data System (NDS) software, developed by the Nutrition Coordinating Center, University of Minnesota, Minneapolis, MN; Food Database version 5A, Nutrient Database version 20. USDA Nutrient Database for Standard Reference. Release 14 at www.nal.usda.gov.fnic.

32. Salmeron J, Manson JE, Stampfer MJ, et al. "Dietary fiber, glycemic load and risk of non-insulin-dependent diabetes mellitus in women." *JAMA* 1997;277(6):472-477.

33. Jacobs DR, Marquart L, Slavin J, Kushi LH. "Whole grain intake and cancer, an expanded review and meta-analysis." *Nutrition and Cancer* 1998;30(2):85-90.

Chatenoud L, Tavani A, La Vecchia C, et al. "Whole grain intake and cancer risk." *Int J Cancer* 1998;77(1):24-28.

34. Brouwer IA, Katan MB, Zock PL, et al. "Dietary alpha-linolenic acid is associated with reduced risk of fatal coronary heart disease, but increased prostate cancer risk: a meta-analysis." *J Nutr* 2004 Apr;134(4): 919-922.

35. Gillman MW, Cuples LA, Millen BE, et al. "Inverse association of dietary fat with development of ischemic stroke in men." *JAMA* 1997; 278:2145-2150.

Iso HM, Stampfer MJ, Manson JE, et al. "Prospective study of fat and protein intake and risk of intraparenchymal hemorrhage in women." *Circulation* 2001;103:856.

Sasaki S, Zhang XH, Kestleloot H. "Dietary sodium, potassium, saturated fat, alcohol and stroke mortality." *Stroke* 1995;26(5):783-789.

36. U.S. Department of Agriculture, Agricultural Research Service. 2005. USDA National Nutrient Database for Standard Reference, Release 18. Nutrient Data Laboratory Home Page, http://www.nal.usda.gov/fnic/foodcomp.

37. Bunyard LB, Dennis KE, Nicklas BJ. "Dietary intake and changes in lipoprotein lipids in obese, postmenopausal women placed on an American Heart Association Step 1 diet." *J Am Diet Assoc* 2002 Jan;102 (1):52-57.

Sharman MJ, Kraemer WJ, Love DM, et al. "A ketogenic diet favorably affects serum biomarkers for cardiovascular disease in normal-weight men." *J Nutr* 2002 Jul;132(7):1879-1885.

Barnard ND, Scialli AR, Bertron P, et al. "Effectiveness of a low-fat vegetarian diet in altering serum lipids in healthy premenopausal women." *Am J Cardiol* 2000 Apr 15;85(8):969-972.

Bemelmans WJ, Broer J, de Vries JH, et al. "Impact of Mediterranean diet education versus posted leaflet on dietary habits and serum cholesterol in a high risk population for cardiovascular disease." *Public Health Nutr* 2000 Sep;3(3): 273-283.

Frolkis J, Pearce GL, Nambi V, et al. "Statins do not meet expectations for lowering low-density lipoprotein cholesterol levels when used in clinical practice." *Am J Med* 2002 Dec 1;113(8):625-629.

Jenkins DJ, Kendall CW, Popovich DG, et al. "Effect of a very-high-fiber vegetable, fruit and nut diet on serum lipids and colonic function." *Metabolism* 2001 Apr;50(4):494-503.

38. Sharman MJ, Kraemer WJ, Love DM, et al. "A ketogenic diet favorably affects serum biomarkers for cardiovascular disease in normal-weight men." *J Nutr* 2002 Jul;132(7):1879-1885.

39. Bemelmans WJ, Broer J, de Vries JH, et al. "Impact of Mediterranean diet education versus posted leaflet on dietary habits and serum cholesterol in a high risk population for cardiovascular disease." *Public Health Nutr* 2000 Sep;3(3):273-283.

40. Bunyard LB, Dennis KE, Nicklas BJ. "Dietary intake and changes in lipoprotein lipids in obese, postmenopausal women placed on an American Heart Association Step 1 diet." *J Am Diet Assoc* 2002 Jan; 102(1):52-57.

41. Barnard ND, Scialli AR, Bertron P, et al. "Effectiveness of a low-fat vegetarian diet in altering serum lipids in healthy premenopausal women." *Am J Cardiol* 2000 Apr 15;85(8):969-972.

42. Frolkis J, Pearce GL, Nambi V, et al. "Statins do not meet expectations for lowering low-density lipoprotein cholesterol levels when used in clinical practice." *Am J Med* 2002 Dec 1;113(8):625-629.

43. Jenkins DJ, Kendall CW, Popovich DG, et al. "Effect of a very-high-fiber vegetable, fruit, and nut diet on serum lipids and colonic function." *Metabolism* 2001 Apr;50(4):494-503.

44. Hu FB, Stampfer MJ, Manson JE, et al. "Frequent nut consumption and risk of coronary heart disease in women: prospective cohort study." *BMJ* 1998 Nov 14;317(7169):1341-1345.

45. Sabate J. "Nut consumption, vegetarian diets, ischemic heart disease risk, and all-cause mortality: evidence from epidemiologic studies." *Am J Clin Nutr* 1999 Sep;70(3 Suppl):500S-503S.

    Albert CM, Gaziano JM, Willett WC, et al. "Nut consumption and decreased risk of sudden cardiac death in the Physicians' Health Study." *Arch Intern Med* 2002 Jun 24;162(12):1382-1387.

46. Hu FB, Stampfer MJ. "Nut consumption and risk of coronary heart disease: a review of epidemiologic evidence." *Curr Atheroscler Rep* 1999 Nov;1(3):204-209.

47. Szapary PO, Wolfe ML, Bloedon LT. "Guggulipid for the treatment of hypercholesterolemia: a randomized controlled trial." *JAMA* 2003; 290(6):765-772.

48. Lottenberg AM, et al. "Food phytosterol ester efficiency on the plasma lipid reduction in moderate hypercholesterolemic subjects." *Arq Bras Cardiol* 2002;79(2):139-142.

    Nestel P, et al. "Cholesterol-lowering effects of plant sterol esters and non-esterfied stanols in margarine, butter and low-fat foods." *Eur J Clin Nutr* 2001;55(12):1084-1090.

49. Aviram M, Rosenblat M, Gaitini D, et al. "Pomegranate juice consumption for 3 years by patients with carotid artery stenosis reduces common carotid intima-media thickness, blood pressure and LDL oxidation." *Clin Nutr* 2004;23(3):423-433.

50. Kim ND, Mehta R, Yu W, et al. "Chemopreventive and adjuvant therapeutic potential of pomegranate (Punica granatum) for human breast cancer." *Breast Cancer Res Treat* 2002;71(3):203-217.

    Kohno H, Suzuki R, Yasui Y, et al. "Pomegranate seed oil rich in conjugated linolenic acid suppresses chemically induced colon carcinogenesis in rats." *Cancer Sci* 2004;95(6):481-486.

Toi M, Bando H, Ramachandran C, et al. "Preliminary studies on the anti-angiogenic potential of pomegranate fractions in vitro and in vivo." *Angiogenesis* 2003;6(2):121-128.

Kawaii S, Lansky EP. "Differentiation-promoting activity of pomegranate (Punica granatum) fruit extracts in HL-60 human promyelocytic leukemia cells." *J Med Food* 2004;7(1):13-18.

51. Aviram M, Dornfeld L, Rosenblat M, et al. "Pomegranate juice consumption reduces oxidative stress, atherogenic modifications to LDL, and platelet aggregation: studies in humans and in atherosclerotic apolipoprotein E-deficient mice." *Am J Clin Nutr* 2000;71(5):1062-1076.

Aviram M, Dornfeld L. "Pomegranate juice consumption inhibits serum angiotensin converting enzyme activity and reduces systolic blood pressure." *Atherosclerosis* 2001;158(1):195-198.

52. Mori-Okamoto J, Otawara-Hamamoto Y, Yamato H, Yoshimura H. "Pomegranate extract improves a depressive state and bone properties in menopausal syndrome model ovariectomized mice." *J Ethnopharmacol* 2004;92(1):93-101.

53. Janikula M. "Policosanol: a new treatment for cardiovascular disease?" *Altern Med Rev* 2002;7(3):203-217.

54. Castano G, Mas R, Fernandez L, et al. "Effects of policosanol and lovastatin in patients with intermittent claudication: a double-blind pilot study." *Angiology* 2003;54(1):25-38.

55. Castano G, Mas R, Fernandez L, et al. "Comparison of the efficacy and tolerability of policosanol with atorvastatin in elderly patients with type 11 hypercholesterolaemia." *Drugs Aging* 2003;20(2):153-163.

56. Tocotrienols. *PDR for nutritional supplements* First Edition 2001; pp. 453-457.

57. Nestel P, Shige H, Pomeroy S, et al. "The n-3 fatty acids eicosapentaenoic acid and docosahexaenoic acid increase systemic arterial compliance in humans." *Am J Clin Nutr* 2002;76(2):326-330.

58. Lemaitre RN, King IB, Mozaffarian D, et al. "N-3 polyunsaturated fatty acids, fatal ischemic heart disease and nonfatal myocardial infarction in older adults: the Cardiovascular Health Study." *Am J Clin Nutr* 2003; 77(2):319-325.

59. Conquer JA. "Supplementation with an algae source of docosahexaenoic acid increases (n-3) fatty acid status and alters selected risk factor for heart disease in vegetarian subjects." *J Nutr* 1996;126(12): 3032-3039.

60. Davis BC, Kris-Etherton PM. "Achieving optimal essential fatty acid

status in vegetarians: Current knowledge and practical implications." *Am J Clin Nutr* 2003;78(3):640S-646S.

61. Conquer JA. "Supplementation with an algae source of docosahexaenoic acid increases (n-3) fatty acid status and alters selected risk factor for heart disease in vegetarian subjects." *J Nutr* 1996;126(12): 3032-3039.

62. Pauleto P, Puato M, Caroli G, et al. "Blood pressure and atherogenic lipoprotein profiles of fish-diet and vegetarian villagers in Tanzania: the Lugaiawa Study." *Lancet* 1996;348:784-788.

63. Spence JD. "Patients with atherosclerotic vascular diseases: how low should plasma homocysteine levels go?" *Am J Cardiovasc Drugs* 2001; 1(2):85-89.

64. Sacco RL, Anand K, Lee HS, et al. "Homocysteine and the risk of ischemic stroke in a triethnic cohort: the Northern Manhattan Study." *Stroke* 2004;35(10):2263-2269.

65. Spence JD. "Nutritional and metabolic aspects of stroke prevention." *Adv Neurol* 2003;92:173-178.

66. Colantuoni C, Rada P, McCarthy J, et al. "Evidence that intermittent, excessive sugar intake causes endogenous opioid dependence." *Obes Res* 2002;10(6):478-88.

Index

A

alcoholism, 28

American College of Cardiology, 15

American Heart Association, xiv, xv, 15, 23, 35, 36, 48, 64

angioplasty, 1, 20-26, 32, 37, 38, 40, 145

animals, cholesterol levels in, 12, 13

anticancer, 79

antioxidant, 5, 12, 28, 50, 53, 60, 61, 66, 69, 80, 121

arachidonic acid, 47, 50

Asian diet, 35

atherosclerosis, 12, 14, 23, 25, 27, 29, 47, 121, 122, 134

B

beans, 9, 28, 44, 51, 52, 65, 74-77, 80-83, 87, 88, 93, 95, 101, 102, 104, 105, 120, 133

blockage, 24, 25, 31, 39, 40, 46, 121

bypass surgery, 1, 20-22, 34, 40

C

cardiac catheterization, 37

CARE Study, 20, 79

cerebral vascular accident CVA, *See* stroke

China, 2, 19, 29

China Study (Cornell-Oxford-China Study), 29, 34, 127

cholesterol-lowering drugs, 4, 14, 20, 116, 119, 120, 122, 131

circulation, 26

clot, 24, 25, 47, 48

D

dairy products, 8, 35, 44-47, 49, 51, 60, 62, 63, 65, 77, 78, 80, 83, 110, 143

Date Nut Pop'ems, 81

dementia, 8, 17, 32, 36, 69, 73, 123, 130, 139

DHA fat, 78, 125, 127, 128

DHA Purity, 123-126

diabetes, xiii, xiv, 8, 10, 16, 17, 44, 52, 56, 60, 64, 69, 73, 74, 136, 139, 141

E

Eat to Live, 8, 9, 38, 39, 41, 59, 63-68, 70, 71, 73, 74, 77, 82, 84, 85, 115, 116, 123, 124, 145, 160

embolic stroke, 2, 55, 56

empty-calorie food, 60

Esselstyn, Caldwell Jr, M.D., 2, 32, 34

exercise, 10, 12, 15, 29, 38, 67, 78, 128, 134, 135, 144, 145

F

flaxseed, 45, 54, 78, 81, 83, 87, 90-92, 111, 120, 127

folate, 61, 130-133

G

garlic, 76, 98, 99, 101-110, 117

grains, 44, 52, 63, 65, 66, 76, 80, 83

green vegetables, 17, 28, 47, 61-63, 75, 83, 96, 128

gugulipid 117, 118

H

Harvard Health Study, 19

HDL cholesterol 6, 7, 9, 41, 46, 47, 64, 65, 67, 71, 122, 125, 126, 128, 129

Healthy Times Newsletter, 85

hemorrhagic stroke, 27, 55-57

high-protein diets, 50, 64

homocysteine, 5, 129-133

hydrogenated fat, 46

I

immune function, 10, 47

infants, cholesterol levels in, 12, 13

inflammatory cells, 25

invasive procedures, 22, 82

J

junk food, 43, 134, 147

L

LDL cholesterol, 2, 12, 13-17, 19-21, 45, 46, 47

LDL Protect, 120, 122-124

LIPID Study, 21

low cholesterol, 26-29, 55

M

Mediterranean diet, 35, 36, 64

monounsaturated fat, 45

N

National Heart, Lung and Blood Institute 8, 10, 14, 40, 115, 119, 123

natural cholesterol-lowering, 8, 10, 14, 40, 115, 119, 123

niacin, 61, 118

nutrient density, 62, 63, 68, 74, 80, 116, 128, 158

nuts and seeds, 45, 54, 78-81, 83, 120, 126, 133

O

oil, 36, 44, 46, 53-55, 64, 66, 68, 69, 78, 80, 120, 124-126

olive oil, 36, 54, 64, 69

optimal cholesterol, 12, 116

Ornish, Dean, M.D., 32, 34

P

pantethine, 118, 119

peripheral vascular disease, 32, 122

plaque, 22-25, 32, 40, 46, 56, 121, 129

policosanol, 122, 123

pomegranate, 89, 91, 92, 99 112, 121-123

processed foods, 43, 44, 46, 52, 53, 60, 65, 80, 120

pulmonary embolisms, 32

R

red rice yeast, 119

regression, 13, 25, 27, 32,

restenosis, 23, 25

rural China, 2, 19, 29

S

salad dressings, 54, 80, 97

saturated fat, xv, 26, 28, 29, 45, 46, 48-51, 56, 61-63, 77, 79, 116, 124, 127, 133, 143

Scandinavian Simvastatin Survival Study, 20

starches, starchy vegetables, 65, 66, 74, 76, 80, 83,109

statins, 6, 20, 21, 60, 64, 119

stenosis, 23-25

sterols and stanols, 120, 121

stroke, 1, 8, 23, 32, 36, 44, 55-57, 60, 122, 123, 125, 139

sweets, 50

T

thrombus, 22

trans fat, 46, 48, 53

triglycerides, 6, 7, 9, 41, 47, 52, 64, 65, 67, 71, 117, 118, 125

U

unsaturated fat, 32

USDA food pyramid, 63

V

vascular dementia, 32

vegan(s), 34, 56, 57, 65, 66, 78, 85, 111, 126, 128, 133

vegetarian, 32, 34, 56, 57, 64-66, 78, 85, 125-128,

venous thrombosis, 32

vitamin B_{12}, 128, 130-133

vitamin B_6, 130

vitamin D, 128

vitamin E, 53, 61

vulnerable plaque, 24, 25

About the Author

Joel Fuhrman, M.D., is a board-certified family physician in private practice specializing in nutritional medicine in Flemington, New Jersey, and an active staff member of Hunterdon Medical Center. A graduate of the University of Pennsylvania School of Medicine, Dr. Fuhrman provides nutritionally oriented medical care to patients as well as nutritional education to graduate students and physicians.

As one of the country's leading experts on nutritional and natural healing, Dr. Fuhrman has been featured in hundreds of magazines and on major radio and television shows, including: "Good Morning America," CNN, "Good Day NY," TV Food Network, and the Discovery Channel's "Second Opinion with Dr. Oz."

Dr. Fuhrman's recommendations are designed for people who desire superior health, effective weight control, and to reverse and prevent disease. His most recent books include *Eat to Live—The Revolutionary Formula for Fast and Sustained Weight Loss* and *Disease-Proof Your Child—Feeding Kids Right*, which describe his methods and results and the science supporting his health and dietary recommendations.

On his website, **www.DrFuhrman.com,** Dr. Fuhrman offers a unique array of supportive services, including a newsletter, customized dietary advice, and a very popular "Ask The Doctor" forum.